Arthur Edward Waite

Elfin Music

An anthology of English fairy poetry

Arthur Edward Waite

Elfin Music
An anthology of English fairy poetry

ISBN/EAN: 9783337240769

Printed in Europe, USA, Canada, Australia, Japan

Cover: Foto ©Thomas Meinert / pixelio.de

More available books at **www.hansebooks.com**

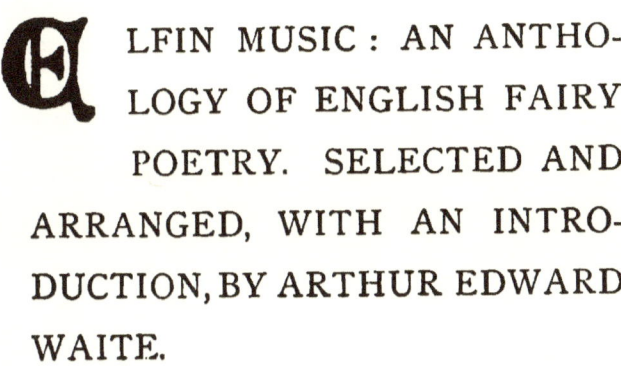

ELFIN MUSIC : AN ANTHO-
LOGY OF ENGLISH FAIRY
POETRY. SELECTED AND
ARRANGED, WITH AN INTRO-
DUCTION, BY ARTHUR EDWARD
WAITE.

"O, list the mystic lore sublime
Of fairy tales of ancient time."
The Ettrick Shepherd.

LONDON
WALTER SCOTT, 24 WARWICK LANE
NEW YORK : THOMAS WHITTAKER
TORONTO : W. J. GAGE AND CO
1888

CONTENTS.

◆

PAGE

INTRODUCTION—Revival of the Romantic element in modern poetry—Origin of the term "Fairy"—Fays of early French literature—Source of the conceptions at the base of English fairy poetry—Huon de Bordeaux—Oberon—Spiritual traditions of Gothic and Celtic nations—Lineage of the fairies—Romance of Orfeo and Heurodis—Stature of the fairies—Their religious faith—The Fairy Queen—Robin Goodfellow—The elfin hierarchies—Romaunt of the Knight Launfal—Value of English fairy poetry—Plan of the present anthology   .   .   ix

THE FOREVIEW.

EDGAR ALLAN POE—Fairyland   8

PRELUDE.

FELICIA HEMANS—Fairies' Recall   .   .   .   7

CONTENTS.

The Fairy Family.

PAGE

EDMUND SPENSER—The Rolls of Elfin Emperours . 11

SIR SIMEON STEWARD—The Faery King . . 13

BEN JONSON—Queen Mab 15

OLD POEM—The Fairy Queen 16

WILLIAM SHAKESPEARE—Queen Mab; Lullaby for
Titania 18, 19

L. E. L.—The Fairy Queen Sleeping . . . 20

OLD POEM—Robin Good-fellow . . . 22

WILLIAM SHAKESPEARE—Puck's Song . . . 26

ROBERT HERRICK—The Fair Temple; Oberon's Feast;
Oberon's Palace . . . 27, 31, 32

THOMAS HOOD—The Water Lady . . . 36

SAMUEL MINTON PECK—The Pixies . . . 37

ANDREW JAMES SYMINGTON—Song of the Water Sprite 38

MARGARET DIXON—A Legend of the Water-Spirit,
called Neckan 40

JAMES HOGG—The Mermaid 42

SARAH WILLIAMS—Song of the Water Nixies . . 46

PHILIP BOURKE MARSTON—Flower Fairies . . 47

THOMAS LAKE HARRIS—Song of the Twilight Fairies . 49

L. E. L.—Fairies on the Sea-shore . . . 50

Chronicles of Fairyland.

MICHAEL DRAYTON—Nymphidia: The Court of Fairy . 55

WILLIAM ALLINGHAM—Prince Brightkin . . 77

J. RODMAN DRAKE—The Culprit Fay . . . 92

CONTENTS. vii

TRAVELS IN FAIRYLAND.

PAGE

SIR WALTER SCOTT—Thomas the Rhymer . . 115
JAMES HOGG—Kilmeny 126
PHILIP JAMES BAILEY—A Fairy Tale . . . 136
A. MARY F. ROBINSON—The Conquest of Fairyland . 149

MEN AND FAIRIES.

WILLIAM SHAKESPEARE—The Approach of Titania . 159
THOMAS PARNELL—A Fairy Tale . . . 161
JOHN LEYDEN—The Elfin King . . . 167
OLD BALLAD—The Young Tamlane . . . 175
WILLIAM NICHOLSON—The Brownie of Blednock 185
JOHN KEATS—La Belle Dame Sans Merci . . 189
THOMAS MOORE—The Mountain Sprite . . 192
SAMUEL LOVER—The Fairy Boy . . . 193
SAMUEL LOVER—The Fairy Tempter . . . 194
MARY HOWITT—The Fairies of the Caldon-Low . 195
CLARENCE MANGAN—The Fairies' Passage . . 198
JAMES TEELING—Thubber-na-Shie; or, The Fairy Well 202
SAMUEL LOVER—The Haunted Spring . . . 205
CLARENCE MANGAN—The Romance of the Fairy Cure . 207
EDWARD WALSH—The Fairy Nurse . . . 209
SAMUEL FERGUSON—The Fairy Thorn ; The Fairy
    Well of Lagnanay 210, 213
CHARLES MACKAY—Kelpie of Corrievreckan . . 216
R. H. HORNE—The Elf of the Woodlands . . 221

viii   *CONTENTS.*

                                                        PAGE
WILLIAM ALLINGHAM—Two Fairies in a Garden   .   239
EDMUND CLARENCE STEDMAN—Elfin Song   .   .   245
GRAHAM R. TOMSON—The Ferlie   .   .   .   248

MISCELLANEOUS.

ROBERT SOUTHEY—The Fountain of the Fairies   .   253
SAMUEL TAYLOR COLERIDGE—Songs of the Pixies   .   254
FELICIA HEMANS—Fairy Favours ; Water Lilies : A
    Fairy Song 258, 26)
L. E. L.—Fantasies   261
ANONYMOUS—The City of Gold   .   .   .   262
WILLIAM ALLINGHAM—The Fairies ; The Maids of
    Elfin Mere 263, 265

EPILOGUE.

RICHARD CORBET—Farewell to the Fairies   .   .   269
FELICIA HEMANS—Fairy Song   270
PHILIP DAYRE—An Invocation   .   .   .   271

INTRODUCTION.

———◆———

THIS volume appears, I trust opportunely, during the initial signs of a revival of that romantic or supernatural element which is the first characteristic of primitive song-craft in every nation, and is, by a select section of discriminating literary critics, now welcomed as the salvation of modern poetry. Independently of this fact, there can be no need for apology in presenting for the first time to the lovers of phantasy an anthology of the fairy poetry which during six centuries has made beautiful by its gracious melody the minor paths of English song. I propose in this brief introduction to consider the Elfin mythology in its connection with poetry, without attempting an actually critical estimate of the literary value of the fairy flights which follow it ; their poetic merit is, for the most part, sufficiently guaranteed by the names which are attached to them—Chaucer and Spenser in

the aurora or day-spring of our literature ; Shake-
speare, Drayton, Herrick, and other masters of
melody in the splendour of its meridian light;
Hogg, Horne, and Allingham at our own epoch of
inspired imaginings.

From the days of Casaubon to Keightley, many
conflicting derivations of the word fairy have been
proposed by rival etymologists. It is now fairly
established that it has come to us from the Latin
fatum, through the Romance languages. A
debased Latin verb, *fatere*, to enchant, was com-
mon in mediæval times, and was naturalised in
Spain, Italy, and Provence. The French form was
faer, féer. Of this verb, says Keightley, in his
masterly *Fairy Mythology*, the past participle is
faé, fé; hence in the romances we continually
meet with *les chevaliers faés, les dames faées*, etc.
From the verb *faér, féer*, to enchant, we are told
by the same authority that the French made a
substantive, *faerié, féerie*, illusion, enchantment,
a word which was considerably extended in its
meaning both before and after its assimilation
into the English language, and which came to be
employed, not only for illusion, but for the land
which was *par excellence* the home of all gramary,
illusion, and *envoutement*, namely, the Land of the
Fairies, for the people who dwell therein, and for
every individual member of the elfin tribe.

It is also established, and by this etymology itself, that the original fairy of Frankish poetry and fiction was simply a female initiated into the mysteries and marvels of magic. Such was the mighty Morgue la Fay, the mystic sister of King Arthur, and such, in unconscious accordance with the original tradition, were those fairies of later French romance who delighted our childhood in the graceful and beautiful stories of Perrault and the Countess d'Aulnoy.

The immediate source of the conceptions which are at the base of English fairy poetry must be evidently sought in the romances and legends of early French chivalry, in such delightful, though comparatively unknown, stories as that of the Paladin Huon de Bordeaux, who was protected in direst extremity, and assisted in the successful prosecution of an almost impossible quest by the divine child Oberon, and then in a glade of dews and sunshine, fenced by the mystic darkness of a Syrian forest, was anointed with supernatural chrism, and instructed in the magical sentences which compel the obedience of elf and gnome and *lutin*, and "crowned King of all Faërie."

Oberon himself, it is true, has a Teutonic origin, and is known to the early Germanic folk-lore by the names of Alberich, Alberon, etc., but the original inspiration of English fairy poetry is

derived, as I have said, through the fairy imagin-
ings of the French metrical romancers. By
these, the supreme monarch of Elfland, who,
despite the supposititious succession of Huon and
his own translation to Paradise, continued to
spread wide his golden rule as in pre-Provençal
days, is represented as a child of four to five
years, indescribable in his beauty, sirenian in voice
and manner, clothed in a robe which sparkled
with all manner of precious stones, and aërially
conveyed in a superb, swan-drawn chariot. His
palace, with its golden roof and diamond spires,
seems to have followed him in his travels, and
thus the Land of Faërie was substantially and for
the time being in that spot wheresoever which
was the tarrying-place of the Grand Master of the
Elfin World.

Side by side with the fays of poetry and chival-
rous history there persisted, in spite of the general
diffusion of Christianity, the old spiritual traditions
of the Gothic and Celtic nations, concerning the
Elves, Trolls, Brownies, malignant or benevolent
dwarfs, gnomes, and generally diminutive beings
gifted with supernatural powers and of an other
than mortal origin. These two hierarchies of
supernal beings were confused in the popular
imagination ; the magical abilities which could
only be painfully acquired by humanity were

identified with the magical prerogatives which were inherent in the natures of Kelpie, Elf, and Ghoul, and the mystical combination produced that new, glorious, and beautiful hierarchy of semispiritual essences which was governed by the elfin Oberon.

The discrepancies in fairy traditions, as preserved in English poetry, may be partly accounted for by the fact of this confusion. We find the most eminent fairy authorities in distinct disagreement on several important points. Spenser, the poet of the elfin world *par excellence*, in his account of the "Rolls of Elfin Emperours," deduces all Faërie from the man-monster created by Prometheus. Shakespeare, on the other hand, refers them to an Indian origin, and the dictionaries of Fairy Mythology, in accordance with this supposition, fix his abode in India, and represent him nightly crossing the intervening seas with inconceivable rapidity to dance in the western moonlight. The oriental origin of magic was generally recognised at a very early period of European gramary ; the original fairies of romance received their wisdom from Persia and from India, and after the transfiguration of the elfin world by the confusion of the several spiritual conceptions already noticed, it is easy to see how an eastern source was attributed to the later fairy lineage.

But on this point it must also be remembered
that the Crusades were undoubtedly the means of
acquainting western poets with the rich fountains
of oriental romance, and that the general similarity
between the Persian Peri and our own fairy, as
well as the substantial identity of many super-
natural fictions which are popular both in the
West and in the East, are a sufficient warrant for
attributing a part of this very transformation to
the glamorous influence of Arabian imaginations.

The classical alternative which is offered by
the poet-chronicler of Fairydom has also a base
in fact.   The Elizabethan age commonly identi-
fied the fairies of Gothic superstition with the
classic nymphs who attended Diana, while the
elfin queen was Diana herself, and was called by
one of the names of that goddess, that is, Titania,
which is found in the metamorphoses of Ovid as
a title of the uranian queen.   The opinion originated
with the romance writers.   Chaucer identifies the
fairies with the inhabitants of the Latin Infernus—

> Pluto that is King of fayrie . . .
> Proserpine and all her fayrie, etc.

The tradition spread wildly, and found during the
early part of the fourteenth century a voice of
poetic beauty in the lovely Scotch fairy-tale of
"Orfeo and Heurodis," which represents the Greek

master of mystical song-craft as a "Kinge in Inglond, who abode in Traciens, or Winchester"—

> The King hadde a quen of priis
> That was y cleped dame Herodis,
> That finest leuedi for the nones
> That might gon on bodi and bones,
> Full of love and of godlinesse
> Ac no man may tell hir fairnesse.

On a certain morn of May, Heurodis, Eurodis, or Eurydice repaired with two of her maidens "to play bi an orchard side," in the neighbourhood of the palace—

> To se the floures sprede and spring,
> And to hear the foules sing.

She fell asleep on the green, and when she awoke it was in a state of frenzy which frightened her virgins away, and they ran back to alarm the whole palace.

She was borne from the orchard to her bed by a long train of knights and ladies, and was visited by the distressed king, whom she informed, amidst great lamentations, that she must go from him—

> As Ich lay this under tide,
> And slepe under an orchard side,
> There come to me to fair knightes
> Wele y armed al to rightes,
> And bad me comen an heighing,

And speke with her lord the king.;
And Ich answered at wordes bold,
Y durst nought, no y nold :
Thai pinkd oghain as thai might driue,
Ther com her king also bliue,
With an hundred knightes and mo,
And damissels an hundred al so ;
Al on snowe white stedes,
As white as milke were her wedes,
Y no seighe yete bifore
So fair creatours y core !
The king hadde a crown on hed,
It nas of silver, no of gold red,
Ac it was of a precious ston ;
As bright as the sonne it schon :
And as son as he to me cam,
Wold Ich, nold Ich, he me nam,
And made me with him ride,
Opon a palfrey by his side,
And brought me to his pallays,
Wele attired in ich ways ;
And schewd me castels and tours,
Rivers, forestes, frith with flours ;
And his riche stedes ichon,
And sith then me brought oghain hom,
Into an owhen orchard,
And said to me afterward :
Loke dame ! to morowe that av be
Right here under this ympe tree ;
And than thou schalt with ous go,
And live with us ever mo,
And yif thou makest ous y let,
Where thou be, thou worst y set,

And to tore thine limes al,
That nothing help the no schal,
And thei thou best so torn,
Yete thou worst with ous y born.

The power of the Fairy King over the royal lady
of earth appears to have been given him in virtue
of her slumber beneath an elvish tree, which,
though growing in her husband's orchard, made
the surrounding grass-plot the property of the
elvish world. Orfeo repaired on the morrow to
the "ympe-tree," accompanied by a thousand
knights, resolved one and all to die, if it were
necessary, ere the queen should go from home ;
but on reaching the fay-bound place Heurodis, in
the midst of the whole company, was spirited
suddenly away. The king in his misery vowed
never again to look upon the face of a woman, and
retired into the wilderness with his harp, which
subdued by its magical melody the fierce beasts
that abounded on every side. This wilderness
eventually proves to be a summer resort of the
Fairy King, where Orfeo beholds distant visions of
elfin hunters, elfin knights, and ladies at the dance,
and then on a certain day of supreme election he
falls into the hands of a joyous bevy of elfin damsels,
among whom he recognises his own Heurodis.
Their mutual emotion betrays him, and she is
carried swiftly away by her companions. Orfeo

B

pursues the bright band with lyre and lamentations;
a rock opens before them; he follows them into it,
and thus reaches Fairy Land.

> He com into a fair countray,
> As bright soonne somers day,
> Smothe and plain and al grene,
> Hill no dale was none ysene.
> Amiddle the lond a castel he seighe,
> Rich and reale and wonder heighe;
> Al the utmust wal
> Was cler and schine of cristal;
> An hundred tours ther were about,
> Degiselich and bataild stout;
> The butrass come out of the diche
> Of rede gold y arched riche;
> The housour was anowed al,
> Of ich maner divers animal;
> Within there wer wide wones
> Al of precious stones,
> The worss piles on to biholde,
> Was al of burnist gold:
> Al that lond was ever light,
> For when it schuld be therk and night,
> The riche stonnes light gonne,
> . Bright as doth at none the sonne:
> No man may tel no thenke in thought
> The riche werk that ther was wrought.

This description corresponds on the whole with
the general drift of legend, which represents the
Land of Faërie to be situated beneath the ground,
so that the true elfin court is a subterranean

pageantry—a point which is commonly ignored by modern fanciful writers.

The castle which Orfeo entered appears to have been a general receptacle for things and persons who had been spirited away from earth, or had in any way suddenly disappeared.

> Ther he seize his owhen wiif,
> Dame Heurodis, his liif liif,
> Slepe under an ympe-tree ;
> Bi her clothes he knewe that it was sche.

He did not, however, at once claim his bride, but repaired to the royal hall where the king and queen of fairyland were seated in a bright and blissful tabernacle, their crowns and vestures almost blinding him by their splendour. Orfeo performs in their presence on his harp, and wins such admiration from the king, that, with Herodian prodigality, he is promised whatever he may demand. The restitution of Heurodis is, of course, the favour in question, and the musician-monarch returns out of Fairyland with a wife beautified more than ever by the gramary of the elfin atmosphere, and, unlike the classical hero, successfully closes his quest by resuming his royal authority.

The entrance of several elements all foreign to each other into the later conception of Fairyland has assisted in the creation of other confusions

besides the conflicting accounts of the elfin
lineage. "Most spirits," says a writer in *Chambers's
Journal*, "could contract and diminish their bulk
at will, but the fairy alone seems to have been
regarded as essentially small in size. The majority
of other spirits, such as dwarfs, genii, etc., are
represented as deformed creatures, whereas the
fairy has almost uniformly been described as a
beautiful miniature of the human being, perfect in
face and form." This statement, however, is not
even generally correct ; it is contradicted con-
tinually in legends and poetry alike. It is evident,
for instance, that the "Queene of Faire Elfland,"
with whom the immortal Rhymer of "bonny
Ercildoune " performed his "mirk night " journey
into Fairyland, was a spirit, at any rate, approach-
ing the common stature of humanity. Such also
were the elfin emperors of Spenser, and such the
fay ladies whom Dryden celebrates in his magnifi-
cent modernised version of Chaucer's "Flower and
the Leaf," and who were simply departed human
beings in a certain state of bondage. The inhabit-
ants of the Elfin World, and generally all classes of
nature-spirits, are poetically depicted in all forms
and sizes at the will of the bard or romancer, and
are sometimes identical with the original human
fairy of the Arthurian and Charlemagne cycles,
sometimes with the diminutive good people of

Gothic lore. These formal discrepancies originated in time a harmonising tradition which well enters into the spirit of fairy mythology. In the fine ballad of " The Young Tamlane," that elfin knight, who had passed from mortality into fairyhood, informs his mistress that he can quit his body when he pleases, and inhabit either earth or air.

> Our shapes and size we can convert
>   To either large or small ;
> An old nut-shell's the same to us
>   As is the lofty hall.

The religion professed in the elfin world is another debated point. According to Chaucer, the book, and bell, and holy water, the matins and other prayers of monks and limitours, had, even in his day, thoroughly exorcised the fairies, and improved them off the face of the earth, a statement which may be true enough in the case of the trolls and the brownies, and other survivals of heathen times.

> In olde dayes of the King Artour,
> Of which that Bretons speken gret honour,
> All was this lond fulfilled of faerie ;
> The elf-quene, with hire joly compagnie
> Danced ful oft in many a grene mede.
> This was the old opinion as I rede ;
> I speke of many hundred yeres ago ;
> But now can no man see non elves mo,
> For now the grete charitee and prayeres

Of limitoures and other holy freres,
That serchen every land and every streme,
As thikke as motes in the sonne beme,
Blissing halles, chambres, kichenes, and boures,
Citees and burghes, castles high, and toures,
Shropes and bernes, shepenes and dairies,
This maketh that ther ben no faeries :
For ther as wont to walken was an elf,
Ther walketh now the limitour himself,
In undermeles and in morweninges,
And sayth his matines and his holy thinges,
As he gotli in his limitatioun.
Women may now go safely up and doun,
In every bush, and under every tree,
Ther is non other incubus but he,
And he ne will don hern no dishonour.

But Bishop Corbet, writing in the days of the Restoration, testified that the fairies "were of the old religion," and that since the advent of Protestantism and Elizabethan glories they had departed hence. Herrick, however, adopts a middle course.

Now, this the fairies would have known,
Theirs is a mixed religion :
And some have heard the elves it call
Part Pagan, part Papisticall.

Intimately associated with the reigning Potentate of Fairyland, the monarch Oberon, and a person of, in some respects, more considerable importance, was the moonlight queen of elves, who is more or less identified by Chaucer, Shakespeare, and the romance of "Orfeo and Heurodis" with the queen of the classical Avernus, Prosperine, but who is distinguished by Drayton from that goddess in his poetic romance of "Nymphidia," and who, as a matter of actual fact, is a combination of several mythological elements.

In the most ancient traditions we have glimpses of a time when this fair and glorious lady alone occupied the faëry throne, and, as in the case of Sire Thopas, was occasionally sought by human lovers. Shakespeare gives her the classical name of Titania, who is commonly identified with Mab, but their characters are sufficiently distinct. The latter, according to Keightley, has completely dethroned Titania, a statement which is scarcely borne out by the facts, for Mab was a person of general celebrity long before the appearance of the "Midsummer Night's Dream," which contains the first mention of the rival sovereign. The herald and messenger of the royal pair was the tricksy sprite indifferently known as Puck, Hobgoblin, and Robin Goodfellow, and who must also perhaps be identified with "the illusory candle-holder," Jack o' Lantern, or Will o' the Wisp, whose fatal phosphorescent light is, in "Paradise Lost," described as

> A wandering fire,
> Compact of unctuous vapour, which the night
> Condenses, and the cold environs round,

Kindled through agitation to a flame,
Which oft, they say, some evil spirit attends,
Hovering and blazing with delusive light,
Misleads the amazed night-wanderer from his way
To bogs, and mires, and oft through pond and pool,
Book the Ninth.

The different hierarchies of fairy spirits who are supposed to be in relation with man may be grouped broadly into three general divisions :—1. Land Fairies. 2. Sea Fairies. 3. Elfin dwellers of the underworld. In the first class will be included such inhabitants of grove and forest as the lovely Korrigan of Brittany, the Moss Folk of Germany, and the Elves proper of English traditional poetry. It will include the fairies of field and meadow such as the Lutin of Normandy, the Little Monk of Neapolitan legends, the Good Neighbours of Scottish lore. It will comprise the domestic fairies who, under the name of Pixies, haunt our Cornish farms and homesteads, the Caledonian Brownie, the Germanic Kobold, and the Niss of Scandinavian legend. The Neckan and Merman are familiar instances of the nature-spirits included in the second division. The elves of the underworld—the trolls, dwarfs, wild-women, and still-folk of Germany, Scandinavia, and Switzerland—are unrepresented in English tradition and poetry, though in most of our early romances the Land of Faerie is supposed to be underground.

Modern imagination has added many supernatural characters to those of ancient legend. Some of its most graceful conceptions—its flower fairies, and sprites of the twilight—are included in this volume.

Besides the story of Orfeo and Heurodis, there are several ancient English metrical romances which are concerned with adventurous quests and travels into Fairyland. Their archaic form and considerable length naturally exclude them from a popular anthology, but this introduction may fitly close with an abstract of one which is singularly beautiful in conception and in high repute among discerning students of our early poetical literature.

The "Romaunt of the Knight Launfal," by Thomas Chestre, is an amplified version of an antique Lay by Marie de France, a Norman poetess, who flourished in the thirteenth century. It is concerned with a " bacheler " named Launfal, who for generosity and *largesse* was made steward at the court of King Arthur, and was chosen by Merlin to bring home the king's bride, Gwennere. The mission was undertaken by the knight—

> But syr Launfal lyked her noght. . . .
> For the lady bar bos of swych word,
> That sche hadde lemanuys under her lord,
> So fele there was noon ende.

After the marriage of Arthur, Launfal took leave of

the court and repaired with two knights to Karl-
youn, where he tarried, making good cheer for a
year's space, till he came to the end of his
resources.   His boon companions then forsook
him, and he fell into great poverty.   In this strait
he borrowed a saddle and bridle from the mayor's
daughter, and rode away westward.

The weather was hot ; he dismounted in a fair
forest, and sat in the shadow of a tree, covering his
worn garments with his mantle.   After a space,
two " gentyll maydenes," wearing kirtles of Indian
sandel and green mantles bordered with gold,
appeared before him.

> Har faces wer whyt as snow on downe,
> Har rode was red, hern ey were browne,
>   I sawe never non swyche ;
> That oon bar of gold a basyn,
> That other a towayle whyt and fyn,
>   Of selk that was good and ryche.

They came to him over the heath ; he greeted
them in all gentleness, while on the part of their
lady, dame Tryamour, they returned his salutation,
and invited him to follow them and speak with her.
He courteously consented, and was conducted to
an honourable pavilion, enriched with gold and
crystal, as well as radiant carbuncles.

> He fond yn the pavyloun
> The Kynges doughter of Olyroun,
>   Dame Tryamour that hyghte,

Her fadyr was Kyng of fayrye,
Of occient fer and nyghe,
  A man of mochell myghte.
In the pavyloun he fond a bed of prys
Theled with purpur bys,
  That semylé was of syghte
Therinne lay that lady gent,
That after Syr Launfal hadde ysent,
  That lessome lemede bryght.
For hete her clothes down sche dede,
Almest to her gerdyl stede,
  Than lay sche uncovert,
She was as whyt as lylye yn May,
Or snow that sneweth yn wynterys day,
  He seyght never non so pert.
The rede rose, whan sche ys newe,
Ayens her rode nes naught of hewe,
  I dare well say yn fert.
Her here schon as gold wyre,
May no man rede her attyre,
  Ne naught well thenke yn hert.

This fay lady informed Launfal that there was no man in all " Christenté," be he king or emperor, whom she loved as much as himself, at which words the knight was inflamed with reciprocal passion,

  And kiste that swete flour ;
    And sat adoun her bysyde,
  And seyde, Swetyng, what so betyde,
    I am to thyn honour.

She tells him that she is acquainted with his present distress, and that if he will truly forsake all women for love of her, she will enrich him inexhaustibly—

> I wyll the yeve an alner,
> Imad of sylk and of gold cler,
> Wyth fayre ymages thre ;
> As oft thou puttest the hond therinne,
> A mark of gold thou schalt wynne,
> In wat place that thou be.

She also promises him her steed Blaunchard and her squire Gyfre, with the additional advantage of her protection by magic art from dangers of war or tournament.

Sir Launfal entered into the agreement ; they supped and slept together, and in the morning she dismissed him, warning him not to boast of his conquest if he wished to retain her love. He returned to Karlyoun, and was presently waited on by ten men, riding upon sumpters, and bearing gold, silver, rich garments, and bright armour. Once more he kept great cheer, but this time it was the poor and unfortunate whom he entertained. His reputation became so great that a tournament was cried in the town to do him honour. The knight closed it with a rich and royal feast which lasted a fortnight. During all this time he was visited nightly by his elfin mistress, but was

destined now to be divided from her by the chal-
lenge of a chevalier in Lombardy, who sent
messengers praying him to cross the sea and take
jousts with him for the honour of his lady.   The
challenge was accepted by Launfal, who repaired
with his steed and his squire to Lombardy, and
achieved so brilliant a victory that he was envied
by "all the lords of Atalye," who vowed revenge
for the defeat of their comrade, but were themselves
slain in great numbers, and the hero returned into
Britain.   The reputation of Launfal reached the
ears of King Arthur, who sent for him.   A feast of
forty days took place, during which the queen took
occasion to avow the passion that had long con-
sumed her for the handsome cavalier who had
conducted her to her bridal home ; but the knight
Launfal, faithful to his fairy mistress, repelled her
advances, and the unexpected indignity, changing
love into hatred, impelled the false wife to denounce
Launfal to her husband as her attempted seducer.
The infuriated monarch vowed his immediate
death, and the unfounded accusation prompted the
knight to boast for the first time of that mysterious
mistress whose supernatural beauties he declared
did utterly transcend and eclipse those of the royal
lady.   On the intervention of certain illustrious
knights—Gawain and Percivall—a respite of a
twelvemonth and a fortnight was granted Launfal

in order that he might produce his mistress, when, if his assertions were seen to be obviously true with regard to her wonderful charms, he should receive his pardon. But the unfortunate lover had broken his compact, he had boasted of his elfin lady, his horse and squire had vanished, the time mentioned drew rapidly to its close ; in truth, the day came when Launfal must pay with his life the forfeit of his supposed crime, and Triamour apparently had left him to his fate.

The knights of the round table, who knew well the character of their queen, began plotting his rescue, and arranging for his flight across the sea, when "ten maydens bright of ble" came to the royal castle, the *avant coureures* of a lady against whose arrival King Arthur courteously appointed his fairest chamber, and then summoned his barons

> For to yeve judgment
> Upon that traytour full of pryde.

Other ten maidens at this juncture rode up and, speaking apart with the monarch, announced the approach of the Lady Triamour. The queen, coming forward, urged her spouse to avenge her on Launfal ; but

> As the quene spak to the kyng,
> The baronns seygh come rydynge
> A damesele alone,

Upon a whyt comely palfrey,
They saw never non so gay
    Upon the grounde gone.
As rose on rip her rode was red,
The her schon upon her hed,
    As gold wyre that schyneth bryght;
Sche hadde a cronne upon her molde,
Of ryche stones and of golde,
    That lossom lemede lyght.
The lady was clad yn purpere palle,
With gentyll body and myddyll small,
    That semely was of syght,
Her mantyll was furryth with whyt ermyn,
Ireversyd jolyf and fyn,
    No rychere be ne myght.
And when Launfal sawe that lady,
To alle the folk he gon crye an hy,
    Both to yonge and olde,
Her, he seyd, comyth my lemman swete,
Sche myghte me of my balys bete,
    Yf that lady wold.

The lady rode into the hall, into the presence of
the King, his queen, and her damsels. The maidens
who had heralded her approach crowded round,
assisting her to dismount. Arthur greeted her, and
she returned his salutation with sweet words. She
informed the monarch of her mission,

        To shere Launfal the knyght,
    That he never, yn no folye,
    Besofte the quene of no drurye,
        By dayes ne by nyght. . . .

He bad naght her, but sche bad hym,
Here lemman for to be.

The king having confessed that she was fairer
and brighter than his wife—

Wyth that dame Tryamour to the quene geth,
And blew on her swych a breth,
  That never eft myght sche se.
The lady lep on hyr palfrey
And bade hem alle have good day,
  Sche nolde no longere abyde ;
Wyth that came Gyfre al so prest,
Wyth Launfal's stede out of the forest,
  And stod Launfal besyde.
The knyght to horse began to sprynge,
Anoon without any lettynge,
  Wyth hys lemman away to ryde ;
The lady took her maydenys achon,
And went the way that sche hadde er gon,
  Wyth solas and wyth pryde.

She carried her lover to a "jolyf ile," called
Olyroun ; and on a certain day in every year you
may still see the horse of the knight Launfal, and
hear his loud neighing, as he goes wearily seeking
his master, who, in all truth, was taken into fairy-
land, and

Seththe saw hym yn thys lond no man,
Ne no more of hym tells y ne can,
  For sothe, wythout lye,

as Thomas Chestre avers in his valedictory lines.

This little volume is devoted to a sweet and delightful section of poetic fancy, and not to the lofty flights of inspired imagination. It is full of felicity and beauty, and though not a tabernacle enshrining the rarest gems, it is a storehouse of dainty devices. If individual poems are occasionally found to fall below the general level of their writers, as perhaps in the case of Herrick, an explanation will possibly be seen in the unserious spirit with which the subject has been too frequently approached by our English poets, who have generally represented a class superior to the superstitions and sometimes to the faiths of the time. In such cases as that of James Hogg, the Ettrick Shepherd, for whom the doctrine of spiritual essences was still true, for whom those elemental intelligences

> Which have their haunts in dale and piny mountain,
> Or forests, by slow stream or tingling brook,

still survived in the "faith of reason," we find the concentrated strength of a vivid and mature imagination devoted to the production of a true fairy poem which is "not for an age but for all time."

A word, in conclusion, must be said on the arrangement of this anthology. The absence of a
c

sufficiently harmonious development of fairy fancy as it is found in our English poetry does not warrant a simple chronological plan ; I have adopted another, which I trust will contribute towards the attractiveness and literary value of the book. It opens with a foreview, or bird's-eye prospect of the fairy country, as it might be beheld by the traveller from without. A prelude follows, which implores the return of its inhabitants into the world of humanity. Then, in the first division there is a particular account of the court, country, and people of Fairyland, of its temples, palaces, and festivals. The second division contains the Chronicles of Fairyland, a series of pleasing poetic romances, where the scene is laid in the Fairy country and the actors are exclusively elfin folk. A third division is devoted to those wonderful and mystical travels or spiritual pilgrimages into Fairyland, which have been occasionally undertaken by favoured and adventurous mortals. The section entitled Men and Fairies comprises those poems and romances in which the different orders of elfin spirits enter into communication with man and mingle in the life of earth, dispensing supernatural benevolence, or working unheard-of woe, according to their various dispositions. Some poems which cannot be included in the foregoing divisions, but deserve by their merits a place in this elfin anthology, are comprised in a miscellaneous section. The work closes with an epilogue, which shows why the fairies have departed, and what are the conditions of their return.

My best thanks are due to Mr. William Allingham for his permission to insert several graceful poems ; to Mr. Philip James Bailey for the use of his mystical " Fairy Tale ; " to Dr. Charles Mackay for similar kindness in respect of his " Kelpie of Corrievreckan," and to a number of recent writers who have generously contributed to the adornment of this collection. The omission of several poems by illustrious contemporary poets, whose copyrights are vigilantly reserved by their publishers, will be viewed by indulgent readers as a matter of necessity, however much it may be regretted.

ARTHUR EDWARD WAITE.

The Foreview.

FAIRYLAND.

DIM vales, and shadowy floods,
And cloudy-looking woods;
Whose forms we can't discover
For the tears that drip all over;
Huge moons there wax and wane—
Again, again, again—
Every moment of the night,
For ever changing places;
And they put out the star-light
With the breath from their pale faces.
About twelve by the moon-dial,
One more filmy than the rest
(A kind which, upon trial,
They have found to be the best)
Comes down—still down—and down
With its centre on the crown
Of a mountain's eminence;
While its wide circumference
In easy drapery falls
Over hamlets, over halls,
Wherever they may be—
O'er the strange woods, o'er the sea,
Over spirits on the wing,
Over every drowsy thing—
And buries them up quite
In a labyrinth of light;
And then, how deep!—O, deep,
Is the passion of their sleep!

FAIRYLAND.

In the morning they arise,
And their moony covering
Is soaring in the skies,
With the tempests as they toss,
Like—almost anything,
Or a yellow albatross.
They use that moon no more
For the same end as before—
Videlicet a tent—
Which I think extravagant :
Its atomies, however,
Into a shower dissever,
Of which those butterflies
Of earth, who seek the skies,
And so come down again,
(Never contented things !).
Have brought a specimen
Upon their quivering wings.

EDGAR ALLAN POE.

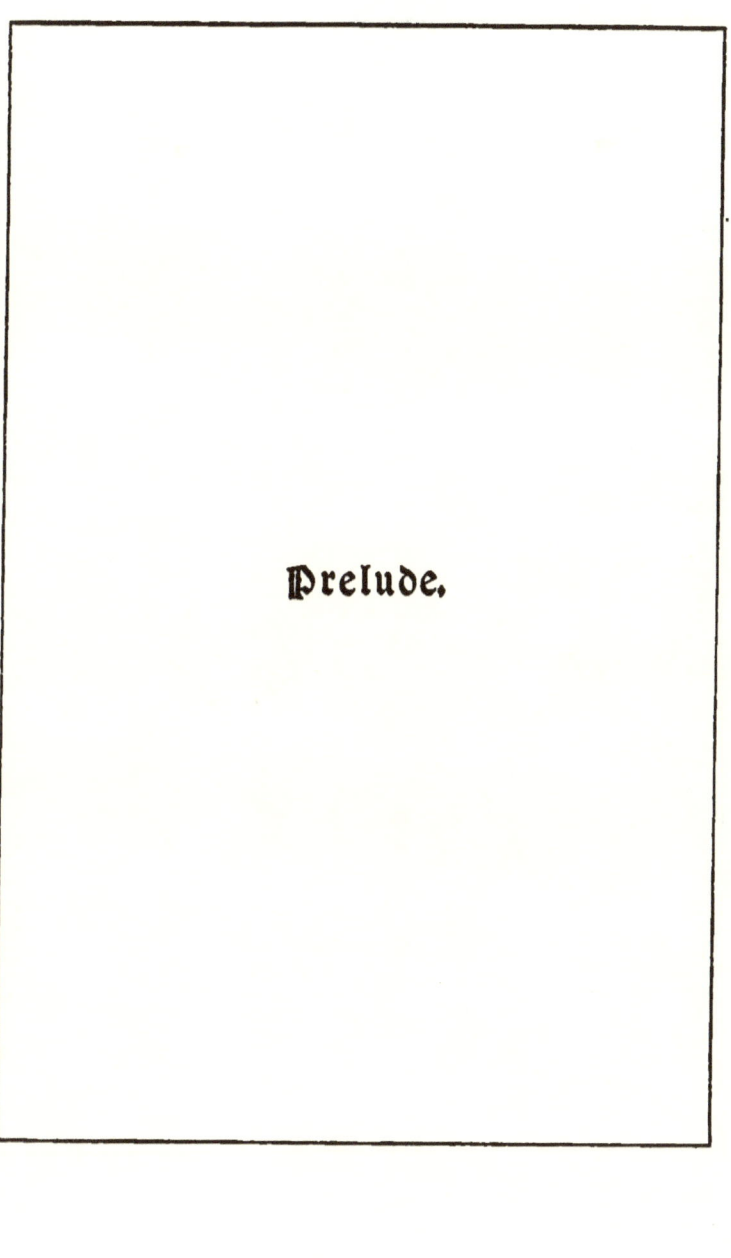

Prelude.

FAIRIES' RECALL.

WHILE the blue is richest
  In the starry sky,
While the softest shadows
  On the greensward lie,
While the moonlight slumbers
  In the lily's urn,
Bright elves of the wild-wood !
  Oh ! return, return !

Round the forest fountain,
  On the river shore,
Let your silvery laughter
  Echo yet once more ;
While the joyous bounding
  Of your dewy feet
Rings to that old chorus :
  "The daisy is so sweet !"

Oberon, Titania,
  Did your starlight mirth
With the song of Avon
  Quit this work-day earth ?
Yet while green leaves glisten,
  And while bright stars burn,
By that magic memory,
  Oh, return, return !

FELICIA HEMANS.

The Fairy Family.

THE ROLLS OF ELFIN EMPEROURS.

PROMETHEUS did create
A man of many parts from beasts deryv'd,
And then stole fire from heven to animate
His worke, for which he was by Jove depryv'd
Of life himselfe, and hart-strings of an ægle ryv'd.

That man so made, he called Elfe, to weet
Quick, the first author of all Elfyn kynd ;
Who, wand'rin through the world with wearie feet,
Did in the Gardins of Adonis find
A goodly Creature, whom he deemd in mynd
To be no earthly wight, but either spright
Or angell, th' author of all woman kynd ;
Therefore a Fay he her according hight,
Of whom all Fayres spring, and fetch their lignage right.

Of these a mighty people shortly grew,
And puissant kinges, which all the world war-rayd,
And to themselves all nations did subdew.
The first and eldest, which that scepter swayd,
Was Elfin ; him all India obayd,
And all that now America men call :
Next him was noble Elfinan, who laid
Cleopolis' foundation first of all,
But Elfiline enclosed it with a golden wall.

His sonne was Elfinelle, who overcame
The wicked Gobbelines in bloody field ;
But Elfant was of most renowned fame,
Who all of crystal did Panthea build :
Then Elfar, who two brethren gyaunts kild,
The one of which had two heads, th' other three ;
Then Elfinor, who was in magick skild ;
He built by art upon the glassy see
A bridge of bras, whose sound heven's thunder seemed
    to be.

He left three sonnes, the which in order raynd,
And all their offspring in their dew descents ;
Even seven hundred princes, which maintaynd
With mightie deeds their sondry governments,
That were too long their infinite contents
Here to record, ne much materiall ;
Yet should they be most famous moniments,
And have ensample, both of martiall
And civil rule to kings and states imperiall.

After all these Elficleos did rayne,
The wise Elficleos ! in great maiestie,
Who mightily that scepter did sustayne,
And with rich spoyles and famous victorie
Did high advaunce the Crown of Faëry.
He left two sonnes, of which fayre Elferon,
The eldest brother, did untimely dy,
Whose empty place the mighty Oberon
Doubly supplide in spousall and dominion.

Great was his power and glory over all,
Which him before that sacred seate did fill,

That yet remains his wide memoriall.
He dying, left the fairest Tanaquill
Him to succeede therein by his last will:
Fairer and nobler liveth none this houre,
Ne like in grace, ne like in learned skill;
Therefore they Glorian call that glorious floure:
Long mayst thou, Glorian! live in glory and great power.

EDMUND SPENSER.

THE FAERY KING.

WHEN the monthly horned queene
Grew jealous that the starrs had seene
Her rising from Endymion's arms,
In rage she threw her misty charmes
Into the bosome of the night,
To dimme theire curious pryeing sight;
Then did the dwarfish Faery elves,
Having first attyr'd themselves,
Prepare to dresse their Oberon King
In light robes fitt for revelling:
With a cobweb shirt more thinne,
Than ever spider since could spin,
Bleacht to the whiteness of the snow,
By the stormie windes that blow
In the vast and frozen ayre
No shirt half so fine, so fayre.
A rich wastcoat they did bring,
Made of the trout-flies gilded wing:
At which his elveship gan to fret,
Swearing it would make him sweat
Even with its weight: he needs would weare

A wastcoat wrought of downy haire,
New shaven from an eunuck's chin,
That pleas'd him well, 'twas wondrous thin ;
The outside of his doublet was
Made of the foure-leav'd, true lov'd, grasse
Chang'd into so fine a glosse,
With the oyle of crispie mosse,
It made a rainbow in the night,
Which gave a lustre passing light :
On every seame there was a lace
Drawne by the unctious snail's slow pace
To which the fin'st, pur'st silver thread
Compar'd, did looke like dull pale lead.
Each button was a sparkling eye
Tane from the speckled adder's frye ;
And for coollness next the skin,
'Twas wᵗʰ white poppey linde wᵗʰin.
His breeches of the fleece was wrought,
Which from Cholchos Jason brought ;
Spun into so fine a yarne,
"No mortal wight might it discerne,"
Weaved by Arachne on her loome,
Just before she had her doome.
A rich mantle he did weare,
Made of tinsell gosameare ;
Beflowered over with a few
Diamond stars of morning dew ;
Dyed crimson in a mayden's blush ;
Lin'd with humble-bee's soft plush.
His cap was all of ladies' love,
So wondrous light that it would move,
If any humming gnat or flie
Buzz'd the air in passing by.
About his necke a wreath of pearle
Dropt from the eyes of some poore girle,
Pinched, because she had forgot

To leave clean water in the pot.
And for's feather he did weare,
Old Nisus' fatall purple haire,
The sword yygirded to his thigh
Was smallest blade of finest rye ;
A payre of buskins they did bringe
Of ye cowladye's corrall winge,
Powdred o'er with spots of jett,
And lin'd wth purple violett.
His belt was made of myrtle leaues,
Pleyted in small curious threavs,
Besett wth amber cowslip's studs,
And fringed about with daysey buds,
In wch his bugle horne was hunge,
Made of the babling Ecchoe's tongue,
Wch sett vnto his moone-burnt lip
He winds, and then his Faeryes skipp ;
At that the lazy drone 'gan sound,
And each did trip a fayrey round.

SIR SIMEON STEWARD.

QUEEN MAB.

THIS is Mab, the mistress Fairy,
That doth nightly rob the dairy,
And can help or hurt the cherning,
As she please without discerning.

She that pinches country wenches,
If they rub not clean their benches,

And with sharper nails remembers
When they rake not up their embers :
But if so they chance to feast her,
In a shoe she drops a tester.

This is she that empties cradles,
Takes out children, puts in ladles :
Trains forth midwives in their slumber,
With a sieve the holes to number ;
And then leads them from her burrows,
Home through ponds and water-furrows.

She can start our Franklin's daughters,
In their sleep, with shrieks and laughters ;
And on sweet St. Anna's night,
Feed them with a promised sight,
Some of husbands, some of lovers,
Which an empty dream discovers.

BEN JONSON.

THE FAIRY QUEEN.

COME, follow, follow me,
You, fairy elves that be ;
Which circle on the greene,
   Come follow Mab, your queene.
Hand in hand let's dance around,
For this place is fairy ground.

When mortals are at rest
And snoring in their nest,
Unheard and unespy'd,
Through key-holes we do glide ;
Over tables, stools, and shelves,
We trip it with our fairy elves.

And, if the house be foul
With platter, dish, or bowl,
Upstairs we nimbly creep,
And find the sluts asleep ;
Then we pinch their arms and thighs ;
None escapes, nor none espies.

But if the house be swept,
And from uncleanness kept,
We praise the household maid,
And duely she is paid :
For we use before we goe
To drop a tester in her shoe.

Upon a mushroomes head
Our table-cloth we spread ;
A grain of rye, or wheat,
Is manchet, which we eat ;
Pearly drops of dew we drink
In acorn cups fill'd to the brink.

The brains of nightingales,
With unctuous fat of snailes,
Between two cockles stew'd,
Is meat that's easily chew'd ;
Tails of wormes and marrow of mice,
Do make a dish that's wonderous nice.

The grasshopper, gnat, and fly
Serve for our minstrelsie ;
Grace said, we dance awhile,
And so the time beguile ;
And if the moon doth hide her head,
The gloe-worm lights us home to bed.

On tops of dewie grasse
So nimbly do we passe
The young and tender stalk
Ne'er bends when we do walk ;
Yet in the morning may be seen
Where we the night before have been.

OLD POEM.

QUEEN MAB.

O THEN, I see, Queen Mab hath been with you.
She is the fairies' midwife, and she comes
In shape no bigger than an agate stone
On the forefinger of an alderman ;
Drawn with a team of little atomies
Athwart men's noses as they iie asleep :
Her wagon spokes made of long spinners' legs ;
The cover, of the wings of grasshoppers ;
The traces, of the smallest spider's web ;
The collars, of the moonshine's watery beams ;
Her whip, of cricket's bone, the lash, of film ;
Her wagoner, a small grey-coated gnat,
Not half so big as a round little worm,

Pricked from the lazy finger of a maid :
Her chariot is an empty hazel nut,
Made by the joiner squirrel, or old grub,
Time out of mind the fairies' coachmakers.
And in this state she gallops night by night,
Through lovers' brains, and then they dream of love ;
On courtiers' knees that dream on court'sies straight ;
O'er lawyers' fingers, who straight dream on fees ;
O'er ladies' lips, who straight on kisses dream.

WILLIAM SHAKESPEARE.

LULLABY FOR TITANIA.

FIRST FAIRY.

You spotted snakes with double tongue,
    Thorny hedgehogs, be not seen ;
Newts, and blind-worms, do no wrong ;
    Come not near our fairy queen.

CHORUS.

Philomel with melody
    Sing in our sweet lullaby ;
Lulla, lulla, lullaby ; lulla, lulla, lullaby !
Never harm, nor spell, nor charm,
    Come our lovely lady nigh !
    So good night, with lullaby.

Second Fairy.

Weaving spiders, come not here ;
    Hence, you long-legg'd spinners, hence ;
Beetles black, approach not near ;
    Worm, nor snail, do no offence.

Chorus.

    Philomel with melody
    Sing in our sweet lullaby ;
Lulla, lulla, lullaby ; lulla, lulla, lullaby !
Never harm, nor spell, nor charm,
    Come our lovely lady nigh !
    So good night, with lullaby.

WILLIAM SHAKESPEARE.

THE FAIRY QUEEN SLEEPING.

SHE lay upon a bank, the favourite haunt
Of the spring wind in its first sunshine hour,
For the luxuriant strawberry blossoms spread
Like a snow-shower there, and violets
Bow'd down their purple vases of perfume
About her pillow,—link'd in a gay ban !
Floated fantastic shapes, these were her guards,
Her lithe and rainbow elves.

We have been o'er land and sea,
Seeking lovely dreams for thee,—
Where is there we have not been
Gathering gifts for our sweet queen ?

We are come with sound and sight
Fit for fairy's sleep to-night ;—
First around thy couch shall sweep
Odours, such as roses weep
When the earliest spring rain
Calls them into life again ;
Next upon thine ear shall float
Many a low and silver note,
Stolen from a dark-eyed maid,
When her lover's serenade,
Rising as the stars gréw dim,
Waken'd her from thoughts of him ;—
There shall steal o'er lip and cheek
Gales, but all too light to break
Thy soft rest,—such gales as hide
All day orange-flowers inside,
Or that, while hot noontide, dwell
In the purple hyacinth bell ;
And before thy sleeping eyes
Shall come glorious pageantries,—
Palaces of gems and gold,
Such as dazzle to behold,—
Gardens, in which every tree
Seems a world of bloom to be,—
Fountains, whose clear waters show
The white pearls that lie below.—
During slumber's magic reign
Other times shall live again ;
First thou shalt be young and free
In thy days of liberty,—
Then again be woo'd and won
By thy stately OBERON.
Or thou shalt descend to earth,
And see all of mortal birth.—
No, that world's too full of care
For e'en dreams to linger there.

But, behold, the sun is set,
And the diamond coronet
Of the young moon is on high
Waiting for our revelry ;
And the dew is on the flower,
And the stars proclaim our hour ;
Long enough thy rest has been,
Wake, TITANIA, wake, our queen !

L. E. L.

ROBIN GOOD-FELLOW.

FROM Oberon, in fairye land,
    The King of ghosts and shadows there,
Mad Robin I, at his command,
    Am sent to view the night-sports here.
        What revell rout
        Is kept about,
    In every corner where I go,
        I will o'ersee,
        And merry bee,
    And make good sport, with ho, ho, ho !

More swift than lightning can I flye
    About this aery welkin soone,
And, in a minute's space, descrye
    Each thing that's done below the moone.
        There's not a hag
        Or ghost shall wag

Or cry, "'Ware Goblins!" where I go,
    But Robin I
      Their feates will spy,
And send them home, with ho, ho, ho!

Whene'er such wanderers I meete,
As from their night-sports they trudge home,
With counterfeiting voice I greete
    And call them on with me to roame
      Thro' woods, thro' lakes,
      Thro' bogs, thro' brakes;
Or else, unseene, with them I go,
      All in the nicke
      To play some tricke
And frolicke it, with ho! ho! ho!

Sometimes I meete them like a man;
    Sometimes, an ox; sometimes, a hound!
And to a horse I turn me can,
    To trip and trot about them round.
      But if, to ride,
      My backe they stride,
More swift than wind away I go,
      O'er hedge and lands,
      Thro' pools and ponds
I whirry, laughing, ho, ho, ho!

When lads and lasses merry be,
    With possets and with juncates fine,
Unseene of all the company,
    I eat their cakes and sip their wine;
      And, to make sport
      I fart and snort,

And out the candles I do blow;
    The maids I kiss;
    They shrieke,—" Who's this?"
I answer nought, but ho, ho, ho!

Yet now and then, the maids to please,
  At midnight I card up their wooll;
And while they sleepe and take their ease,
  With whee to threads their wax I pull.
    I grind at mill
    Their malt up still;
I dress their hemp, I spin their tow.
    If any 'wake
    And would me take,
I wend me; laughing, ho, ho, ho!

When house or harth doth sluttish lye,
  I pinch the maidens black and blue;
The bed-clothes from the bedd pull I,
  And lay them naked all to view.
    'Twixt sleepe and wake
    I do them take,
And on the key-cold floor them throw.
    If out they cry,
    Then forth I fly,
And loudly laugh out, ho, ho, ho!

When any need to borrowe ought,
  We lend them what they do require,
And for the use demand we nought,
  Our owne is all we do desire.
    If to repay
    They do delay,

Abroad amongst them then I go,
　　And night by night
　　I them affright
With pinchings, dreames, and ho, ho, ho !

When lazie queans have nought to do
　But study how to cog and lye,
To make debate and mischief too,
　'Twixt one another secretlye,
　　I marke their gloze,
　　And it disclose
To them whom they have wronged so ;
　　When I have done
　　I get me gone,
And leave them scolding, ho, ho, ho !

When men do traps and engins set
　In loop holes, where the vermine creep,
Who from their foldes and houses get
　Their ducks and geese, and lambes and sheepe,
　　I spy the gin,
　　And enter in,
And seeme a vermine taken so ;
　　But when they there
　　Approach me neare,
I leap out laughing, ho, ho, ho !

By wells and rills, in meadowes greene,
　We nightly dance our hey-day guise,
And to our fairye king and queene
　We chant our moonlight minstrelsies.
　　When larks 'gin sing,
　　Away we fling ;

And babes new borne steal as we go,
And elfe in bed
We leave instead,
And wend us laughing, ho, ho, ho!

From hag-bred Merlin's time have I
Thus nightly revell'd to and fro,
And for my pranks men call me by
The name of Robin Good-fellow.
Fiends, ghosts, and sprites
Who haunt the nightes,
The hags and goblins do me know,
And beldames old
My feats have told,
So *vale, vale;* ho, ho, ho!

OLD POEM.

PUCK'S SONG.

OVER hill, over dale,
Through bush, through brier,
Over park, over pale,
Thorough flood, thorough fire,
I do wander everywhere,
Swifter than the moone's sphere;
And I serve the fairy queen,
To dew the orbs upon the green:
The cowslips tall her pensioners be;
In their gold coats spots you see;
Those be rubies, fairy favours;
In those freckles live their savours:
I must go seek some dewdrops here,
And hang a pearl in every cowslip's ear.

WILLIAM SHAKESPEARE.

THE FAIR TEMPLE;

OR, OBERON'S CHAPEL.

A WAY enchased with glass and beads
There is, that to the chapel leads,
Whose structure, for his holy rest,
Is here the Halcyon's curious nest :
Into the which who looks, shall see
His temple of idolatry,
Where he of godheads has such store,
As Rome's Pantheon had not more.
His house of Rimmon this he calls,
Girt with small bones, instead of walls.
First, in a niche, more black than jet,
His idol-cricket there is set ;
Then in a polished oval by,
There stands his idol-beetle-fly :
Next, in an arch, akin to this,
His idol-canker seated is :
Then in a round, is placed by these
His golden god, Cantharides.
So that where'er ye look, ye see
No capital, no cornice free,
Or frieze, from this fine frippery.
Now, this the fairies would have known,
Theirs is a mixed religion :
And some have heard the elves it call
Part Pagan, part Papisticall.
If unto me all tongues were granted,
I could not speak the saints here painted.
Saint Tit, Saint Nit, Saint Is, Saint Itis,
Who 'gainst Mab's state placed here right is.
Saint Will-o'-th'-Wisp, of no great bigness,
But alias called here *fatuus ignis*.

Saint Frip, Saint Trip, Saint Fill, Saint Fillie,
Neither those other saintships will I
Here go about for to recite
Their number, almost infinite,
Which, one by one, here set down are
In this most curious calendar.
First, at the entrance of the gate,
A little puppet-priest doth wait,
Who squeaks to all the comers there,
" Favour your tongues, who enter here,
Pure hands bring hither, without stain."
A second pules, " Hence, hence, profane."
Hard by, i' th' shell of half a nut,
The holy water there is put ;
A little brush of squirrels' hairs,
Composed of odd, not even pairs,
Stands in the platter or close by
To purge the fairy family.
Near to the altar stands the priest,
There off'ring up the Holy Grist ;
Ducking in mood and perfect tense,
With (much good do't him) reverence.
The altar is not here four-square,
Nor in a form triangular ;
Nor made of glass, or wood, or stone,
But of a little transverse bone
Which boys and bruckelled children call
(Playing for points and pins) cockall.
Whose linen drapery is a thin,
Subtile, and ductile codlin's skin :
Which o'er the board is smoothly spread
With little seal-work damaskèd.
The fringe that circumbinds it, too,
Is spangle work of trembling dew,
Which, gently gleaming, makes a show,
Like frost-work glitt'ring on the snow.

Upon this fetuous board doth stand
Something for shew-bread, and at hand
(Just in the middle of the altar)
Upon an end, the Fairy-psalter,
Graced with the trout-fly's curious wings,
Which serve for watchet ribbonings.
Now, we must know, the elves are led
Right by the Rubric, which they read:
And if report of them be true,
They have their text for what they do,
Ay, and their book of canons too.
And, as Sir Thomas Parson tells,
They have their Book of Articles:
And if that Fairy Knight not lies,
They have their Book of Homilies;
And other Scriptures, that design
A short, but righteous discipline.
The basin stands the board upon
To take the Free Oblation,
A little pin-dust, which they hold
More precious than we prize our gold;
Which charity they give to many
Poor of the parish, if there's any.
Upon the ends of these neat rails,
Hatched with the silver-light of snails,
The elves, in formal manner, fix
Two pure and holy candlesticks,
In either which a small tall bent
Burns for the altar's ornament.
For sanctity, they have, to these,
Their curious copes and surplices
Of cleanest cobweb, hanging by
In their religious vestery.
They have their ash-pans and their brooms,
To purge the chapel and the rooms;
Their many mumbling mass-priests here,

And many a dapper chorister.
Their ushering vergers, here likewise,
Their canons and their chanteries :
Of cloister monks they have enow,
Ay, and their abbey-lubbers too.
And if their legend do not lie,
They much affect the Papacy ;
And since the last is dead, there's hope
Elve Boniface shall next be Pope.
They have their cups and chalices,
Their pardons and indulgences ;
Their beads of nuts, bells, books, and wax,
Candles, forsooth, and other knacks ;
Their holy oil, their fasting spittle,
Their sacred salt here, not a little.
Dry chips, old shoes, rags, grease, and bones,
Besides their fumigations,
To drive the devil from the cod-piece
Of the friar, of work an odd piece,
Many a trifle, too, and trinket,
And for what use, scarce man would think it.
Next then, upon the chanter's side
An apple's core is hung up dried,
With rattling kernels, which is rung
To call to morn and even-song.
The saint, to which the most he prays
And offers incense nights and days,
The lady of the lobster is,
Whose foot-pace he doth stroke and kiss,
And humbly chives of saffron brings,
For his most cheerful offerings.
When, after these, he's paid his vows,
He lowly to the altar bows :
And then he dons the silkworms shed,
Like a Turk's turban on his head,
And reverently departeth thence,

Hid in a cloud of frankincense;
And by the glow-worm's light well-guided,
Goes to the feast that's now provided.

ROBERT HERRICK.

OBERON'S FEAST.

A LITTLE mushroom-table spread,
After short prayers they set on bread,
A moon-parched grain of purest wheat,
With some small glitt'ring grit, to eat
His choice bits with; then in a trice
They make a feast less great than nice.
But all this while his eye is served,
We must not think his ear was starved;
But that there was in place to stir
His spleen, the chirring grasshopper,
The merry cricket, puling fly,
The piping gnat for minstrelsy.
And now, we must imagine first,
The elves present, to quench his thirst,
A pure seed-pearl of infant dew,
Brought and besweetened in a blue
And pregnant violet; which done,
His kitling eyes begin to run
Quite through the table, where he spies
The horns of papery butterflies,
Of which he eats; and tastes a little
Of that we call the cuckoo's spittle.
A little fuz-ball puddling stands
By, yet not blessed by his hands,
That was too coarse; but then forthwith
He ventures boldly on the pith

Of sugared rush, and eats the sagg
And well be-strutted bee's sweet bag ;
Gladding his palate with some store
Of emmets' eggs; what would he more,
But beards of mice, a newt's stewed thigh,
A bloated earwig, and a fly ;
With the red-capped worm, that's shut
Within the concave of a nut,
Brown as his tooth.   A little moth,
Late fattened in a piece of cloth ;
With withered cherries, mandrake's ears,
Mole's eyes ; to these the slain stag's tears;
The unctuous dewlaps of a snail,
The'broke-heart of a nightingale
O'ercome in music ; with a wine
Ne'er ravished from the flattering vine,
But gently pressed from the soft side
Of the most sweet and dainty bride,
Brought in a dainty daisy, which
He fully quaffs up to bewitch
His blood to height ; this done, commended
Grace by his priest ; the feast is ended.

Robert Herrick.

OBERON'S PALACE.

Full as a bee with thyme, and red
As cherry harvest, now high fed
For lust and action ! on he'll go
To lie with Mab, though all say no.
Lust has no ears ; he's sharp as thorn,
And fretful, carries hay in 's horn,
And light'ning in his eyes ; and flings

Among the elves, if mov'd, the stings
Of pettish wasps; well know his guard,
Kings, though they're hated, will be feared.
Wine led him on. Thus to a grove,
Sometimes devoted unto love,
Tinselled with twilight, he and they
Led by the shine of snails, a way
Beat with their num'rous feet, which by
Many a neat perplexity,
Many a turn, and many a cross-
Track, they redeem a bank of moss
Spongy and swelling, and far more
Soft then the finest Lemster ore :
Mildly disparkling, like those fires
Which break from the enjewelled tyres
Of curious brides; or like those mites
Of candied dew in moony nights.
Upon this convex, all the flowers
Nature begets by th' sun and showers,
Are to a wild digestion brought,
As if Love's sampler here was wrought;
Or Citherea's ceston, which
All with temptation doth bewitch.
Sweet airs move here, and more divine
Made by the breath of great-eyed kine,
Who, as they low, empearl with milk
The fern-leav'd grass, or moss like silk.
The breath of monkeys met to mix
With musk-flies, are th' aromatics
Which cense this arch ; and here and there,
And farther off, and everywhere
Throughout that brave mosaic yard,
Those picks or diamonds in the card,
With pips of hearts, of club and spade,
Are here most neatly interlaid.
Many a counter, many a die,

Half rotten and without an eye,
Lies hereabouts ; and for to pave
The excellency of this cave,
Squirrels' and children's teeth late shed,
Are neatly here enchequerèd,
With brownest toadstones, and the gum
That shines upon the bluer plum.
The nails fall'n off by whit-flows : Art's
Wise hand enchasing here those warts
Which we to others (from ourselves)
Sell, and brought hither by the elves.
The tempting mole, stol'n from the neck
Of the shy virgin, seems to deck
The holy entrance ; where within,
The room is hung with the blue skin
Of shifted snake ; enfriezed throughout
With eyes of peacocks' trains, and trout-
Flies' curious wings ; and these among
Those silver-pence, that cut the tongue
Of the red infant, neatly hung.
The glow-worm's eyes, the shining scales
Of silv'ry fish, wheat-straws, the snail's
Soft candle-light, the kitling's eyne,
Corrupted wood, serve here for shine.
No glaring light of bold-faced day,
Or other over-radiant ray,
Ransacks this room ; but what weak beams
Can make reflected from these gems,
And multiply ; such is the light,
But ever doubtful, day or night.
By this quaint taper-light, he winds
His errors up ; and now he finds
His moon-tanned Mab, as somewhat sick,
And, love knows, tender as a chick.
Upon six plump dandélions, high-
Reared, lies her elvish majesty,

Whose woolly bubbles seemed to drown
Her Mabship in obedient down ;
For either sheet was spread the caul
That doth the infant's face enthral,
When it is born, by some enstyled
The lucky omen of the child ;
And next to these, two blankets o'er-
Cast of the finest gossamer ;
And then a rug of carded wool,
Which, sponge-like, drinking in the dull
Light of the moon, seemed to comply,
Cloud-like, the dainty deity.
Thus soft she lies ; and overhead
A spinner's circle is bespread
With cobweb curtains, from the roof
So neatly sunk, as that no proof
Of any tackling can declare
What gives it hanging in the air.
The fringe about this, are those threads
Broke at the loss of maidenheads ;
And all behung with these pure pearls
Dropt from the eyes of ravished girls
Or writhing brides, when panting they
Give unto love the straighter way.
In music now he has the cries
Of fainèd-lost virginities ;
The which the elves make to excite
A more unconquered appetite.
The king's undressed ; and now upon
The gnat's watchword the elves are gone.
And now the bed, and Mab possessed
Of this great-little kingly quest,
We'll nobly think what's to be done,
He'll do no doubt.   This flax is spun.

ROBERT HERRICK.

THE WATER-LADY.

ALAS, the moon should ever beam
  To show what man should never see !——
I saw a maiden on a stream,
  And fair was she !

I staid awhile, to see her throw
  Her tresses back, that all beset
The fair horizon of her brow
  With clouds of jet.

I staid a little while to view
  Her cheek, that wore in place of red,
The bloom of water, tender blue,*
  Daintily spread.

I staid to watch, a little space,
  Her parted lips if she would sing ;
The waters closed above her face
  With many a ring.

And still I staid a little more,
  Alas ! she never comes again !
I throw my flowers from the shore,
  And watch in vain.

I know my life will fade away,
  I know that I must vainly pine,
For I am made of mortal clay,
  But she's divine.

THOMAS HOOD.

* In a little water-colour sketch by Severn, given to Mrs.
Hood by Keats, the nymph's complexion was of a pale blue.

THE PIXIES.

THE frost hath spread a shining net
  Where last the autumn roses blew ;
On lake and stream a seal is set
  Where floating lilies charmed the view ;
  So silently the wonder grew
Beneath pale Dian's mystic light,
  I know my fancies whisper true,
The Pixies are abroad to-night.

When at the midnight chime are met
  Together elves of every hue,
I trow the gazer will regret
  That peers upon their retinue ;
  For limb awry and eye askew
Have oft proclaimed a fairy's spite —
  Peep slyly, gallants, lest ye rue,
The Pixies are abroad to-night.

'Tis said their forms are tiny, yet
  All human ills they can subdue,
Or with a wand or amulet
  Can win a maiden's heart for you ;
  And many a blessing know to strew
To make the way to wedlock bright ;
  Give honour to the dainty crew,
The Pixies are abroad to-night.

ENVOY.

Prince, e'en a prince might vainly sue,
  Unaided by a fairy's might ;
Remember Cinderella's shoe,
  The Pixies are abroad to-night.

SAMUEL MINTON PECK.

SONG OF THE WATER SPRITE.

THE weary sun, all goldën red,
    Sinks in the sea ;
All fiery glows his ocean bed—
    There seek me ;
For there, my floating tresses lave
In the golden fires of the crystal wave,
    For ever free !

When Vesper first peers through the sky
    O'er wild Tīree,
And twinkling darts her light from high—
    There find me ;
The clear air nerves my gossamer wing,
And I love to hear the star-sprites sing,
    For ever free !

The mildly radiant Queen of Night
    Dreams o'er the sea,
And bathes the deep in silv'ry light—
    There seek me ;
For there I skim her watery glass,
And I merrily watch each spirit pass,
    For ever free !

I love the Sun—I love the Moon—
    So fair to see ;
I love the little twinkling stars,
    And they love me ;
I, too, love my emerald home,
With its coral cells 'neath the sparkling foam,
    For ever free !

For there, we lightly trip around
    The coral tree,
And quickly beat the pearly ground
    All merrily :
While o'er us, as we gaily sing,
All the crystal domes with music ring,
    For ever free !

When sun, or stars, are shining bright
    Down through the sea,
When pure domes flushed in sunset light
    Change gloriously,
We play with murmuring rose-lipp'd shells,
Or we sail a-down clear waterfalls,
    For ever free !

We hear, in each cool sparry cave,
    Plaint melody
Sung by the mermaids of the wave,
    Æōlianly !
While ocean's coral groves around,
With the witching syren-notes resound,
    For ever free !

Hark ! hark ! the sweet-voiced choir renew
    Their symphony !
All quivering with a rainbow hue
    In ecstasy,
Our spangled wings now waft us high,
Through the mazy paths of the starry sky,
    For ever free !

            ANDREW JAMES SYMINGTON.

A LEGEND OF THE WATER-SPIRIT CALLED NECKAN.

DARK and deep and calm as night
  Flows the stream along ;
Quiet in the evening light,
  As love's fulness strong
Flowing, flowing, flowing on
Swift as sweet days come and gone,
Low murmuring like Eternity,
Softly step two children bright,
Hearkening for the Water-Sprite,
Nigh unto the alder-tree
Where at evening singeth he
As he doth sing to-night,
Floating on the azure tide
Fairer than an earthly bride.
While the river flows along,
Hearken to the spirit's song :
      " Softly falls the summer
        Over all the land,
      Softly flows the river
        Past its mossy strand,
Over-arched by wild-rose bowers,
Clustered with the woodbine flowers
Hanging down their fragrant tresses
Over shady cool recesses,
Where the water-lilies gleam
Tranquil on the moving stream.
Deep beneath, the spirits glide
Who know not sorrow, hate, nor pride ;
Loving earth with its fair things,
Mountain and valley and sunny lea,
But most the rivers so pure and free,

Sparkling fountains, secret springs,
Dewy flowers in radiant bloom,
Morning glories, midnight gloom,
Loving all things pure and bright
With unspeakable delight.
Learning from the starry skies
Everlasting mysteries."
Sudden ceased both lyre and song
(Softly flowed the stream along),
For thus spake those children young :
" Oh, Neckan, what availeth thee
To sing and play so gloriously
In perfect exultation ?
What avail the starry skies,
Or the splendour of thine eyes,
Or the unsealed mysteries ?
For thee is no salvation ! "
Weeping sore the Spirit threw
Far his golden-stringèd lyre,
Piteous wailing, wild and shrill,
Sank he in the waters blue ;
In a fairy-ring of fire
Once they flashed and then were still.
Homeward turned the children bright
Through the meadows green and wide,
Soon their father's knee beside
Told they of the Water-Sprite.
Grave he heard them, answering then
" Nay, my children, ye were wrong
Thus to mar the Spirit's song.
Hasten to-morrow to the glen
When the light is fair and dim
That the sunset giveth,
Tell the Spirit that for him,
Him too the Saviour liveth."
On the morrow when the sun

To the western gates had run,
Forth there stepped those children bright
Hearkening for the Water-Sprite.
Soon they heard him wailing low
In his sad extreme of woe,
Underneath the alder-tree
Weeping in his misery.
Softly drew the children near,
Softly spake : " Oh, Spirit, hear,
Our sire this comfort giveth :
God has sent His Son to be
The World's Redeemer, then for thee
See ! the Redeemer liveth ! "
Then the Spirit wept no more,
Golden-stringèd lyre he strung,
Soon melodious echoes rung
From the farther, wooded shore.
Gloriously he played and sung,
Whilst the sun withdrew his light,
Slowly rose behind the trees
Orion and the Pleiades,   [Sprite.
And still went singing on the joyful Water

MARGARET DIXON.

THE MERMAID.

" OH, where won ye, my bonny lass,
    Wi' look sae wild an' cheery ?
There's something in that witching face
    That I lo'e wonder dearly."

"I live where the harebell never grew,
    Where the streamlet never ran,
Where the winds o' Heaven never blew—
    Now find me gin you can."

"'Tis but your wild an' wily way,
  The gloaming makes you eerie,
For ye are the lass o' the Braken-Brae,
  An nae lad maun come near ye :

" But I am sick, an' very sick,
  Wi' a passion strange and new,
For ae kiss of thy rosy cheeks
  And lips o' coral hue."

    .   ·   ·   ·   ·

" Go, hie you from this lonely brake,
  Nor dare your walk renew ;
For I'm the Maid of the Mountain Lake,
  An' I come wi' the falling dew."

" Be you the maid of the Crystal Wave,
  Or she of the Braken Brae ;
One tender kiss I mean to have ;
  You shall not say me nay.

" For beauty's like the daisy's vest,
  That shrinks from the early dew ;
But soon it opes its bonny breast,
  An' sae may it fare wi' you."

" Kiss but this hand, I humbly sue,
  Ev'n there I'll rue the stain ;
For the breath of men will dim its hue,
  It will ne'er be pure again.

"For passion's like the burning beal
   Upon the mountain's brow,
That wastes itself to ashes pale,
   And sae will it fare with you."

"Oh, mother, mother, make my bed,
   And make it soft and easy;
And with the cold dew bathe my head,
   For pains of anguish seize me:

"Or stretch me in the chill blue lake,
   To quench this bosom's burning;
An' lay me by yon lonely brake,
   For hope there's none returning.

"I've been where man should not have been,
   Oft in my lonely roaming;
And seen what man should not have seen
   By greenwood in the gloaming.

"Oh, passion's deadlier than the grave,
   A' human things undoing;
The Maiden of the Mountain Wave
   Has lured me to my ruin!"

'Tis now an hundred years an' more,
   An' all these scenes are over,
Since rose his grave on yonder shore
   Beneath the wild wood cover;

An' late I saw the Maiden there,
    Just as the daylight faded,
Braiding her locks o' gowden hair,
    And singing as she braided :

MERMAID'S SONG.

Lie still, my love, lie still and sleep,
    Long is thy night of sorrow ;
The Maiden of the mountain deep
    Shall meet you on the morrow.

But oh, when shall that morrow be
    That my true love shall waken ?
When shall we meet, refined an' free,
    Amid the moorland braken ?

Full low and lonely is thy bed,
    The worm even flies thy pillow ;
Where now the lips, so comely red,
    That kissed me 'neath the willow?

Oh, I must laugh, do as I can,
    Ev'n mid my song of mourning,
At all the fuming freaks of man,
    To which there's no returning.

Lie still, my love, lie still and sleep—
    Hope lingers o'er thy slumber ;
What though thy years beneath the steep
    Should all its stones outnumber?

Though moons steal o'er an' seasons fly
    On time's swift wing unstaying,
Yet there's a spirit in the sky,
    That lives o'er thy decaying.

In domes beneath the water-springs,
　No end hath my sojourning ;
An' to this land of fading things
　Far hence be my returning ;

For spirits now have left the deep,
　Their long last farewell taken :
Lie still, my love, lie still an' sleep,
　The day is near the breaking !

When my loved flood from fading day
　No more its gleam shall borrow,
Nor heath-fowl from the moorland grey
　Bid the blue dawn good-morrow ;

The Mermaid o'er thy grave shall weep,
　Without one breath of scorning :
Lie still, my love, lie still an' sleep,
　And fare thee well till morning !

JAMES HOGG.

SONG OF THE WATER NIXIES.

By the ripple, ripple of the shallow sea,
　　　By the rocky sea,
　　　By the hollow sea,
We have built a giant windmill, with its long arms free,
　　　And it grinds, that we
　　　May not hungry be.
With a rumble and a roar, sounding all along the shore,
We should vanish and should perish if our wheel were
　heard no more.

Little hopes of fisher maidens in the far-off town,
   In our wheel go down,
   Evermore go down,
For the fisher lads that hold them in the deep sea
 drown,
   By our grinding drown,
   For our pleasures drown.
Rend the garment from the soul; let it go, we care not
 where;
What do mortals want with spirit? 'Tis the bodies that
 are fair.

Out beyond the green horizon lurks the vengeful day,
   Lurks the fateful day,
   Lurks the hateful day.
When the winds shall cease to help us in our shark-like
 play,
   When our calm cold sway
   Shall have passed away,
When the wreckers and the wrecked both at peace shall
 be, —   [sea.
When the threat shall be fulfilled, and there be no more

       Sarah Williams.

FLOWER FAIRIES.

Flower Fairies have you found them,
 When the summer dusk is falling,
With the glow-worms all around them,
 Have you heard them softly calling?

Calling through your garden spaces
 Notes like fairy bells set ringing,
Heard from out enchanted places
 Whence the fairy bees come winging?

Silent stand they through the noonlight
　　In their flower shapes fair and quiet,
But they quit them in the moonlight,
　　In its beams to sing and riot.

I have heard them, *I* have seen them,
　　From their petals light-like raying,
And the trees would fain have been them,
　　The great trees too old for playing.

Hundreds of them altogether,
　　Flashing flocks of flying fairies,
Crowding through the summer weather,
　　Seeking where the coolest air is.

And they tell the trees that know them,
　　As upon their boughs they hover,
Of the things that chance below them,
　　How the rose has a new lover.

And the roses laugh, protesting
　　That the lilies are as fickle ;
Then they look where birds are nesting,
　　And their feathers softly tickle.

Then away they all go sweeping,
　　Having had their fill of gladness,
But the trees, their night-watch keeping,
　　Feel a tender, loving sadness.

For *they* know of bleak December,
　　When each bough to pain left bare is,
When they only shall remember
　　Those bright visitings of fairies.

When the roses and the lilies
  Shall be gone to come back never,
To a land where all so still is
  That they sleep and sleep for ever.

PHILIP BOURKE MARSTON.

SONG OF THE TWILIGHT FAIRIES.

VESTAL moon, vestal moon,
  Star of Love's delight,
Rise, and gild our festal noon –
  Noon of Fairy-night.
Vestal moon, vestal moon,
  Up the golden height,
Thou art rising to thy noon—
  We to Love's delight.
Fairies hide in cowslip bells
  Through the garish light ;
Naiads rest in purple shells,
  By the sea-marge bright.

Fairy-Queen, appear, appear,
  From thy citron nest ;
Wake, O wake ! come, Sweet, for here
  Shines the moonlight blest.
Golden Fairies in the sun
  Wind their elfin horn,
Where the dancing streamlets run,
  And the Day is born.
Silver fairies haunt the night
  When the Sun's asleep ;
Azure Fays the heavenly height,
  'Mid the starry sheep.

Fays of Silver, Gold, and Blue
 Wake to Love's delight ;
Drink your fill of sweet May-dew,
 Chase the star-flakes bright.
Lo ! we come, we come, we come,
 From the foxglove bells,
Some from golden brake, and some
 From the asphodels.
Vestal moon, vestal moon,
 From your golden height,
Gaze through all the fairy noon
 On our Love's delight.

THOMAS LAKE HARRIS.

FAIRIES ON THE SEA-SHORE.

First Fairy. My home and haunt are in every leaf
Whose life is a summer day bright and brief—
I live in the depths of the tulip's bower,
I wear a wreath of the cistus flower,
I drink the dew of the blue harebell,
I know the breath of the violet well,
The white and the azure violet ;
But I know not which is the sweetest yet,
I have kiss'd the cheek of the rose,
I have watch'd the lily unclose,
My silver mine is the almond tree,
Who will come dwell with flower and me?

Chorus of Fairies.   Dance we our round, 'tis a summer
  night,
And our steps are led by the glow-worm's light.

Second Fairy.   My dwelling is in the serpentine
Of the rainbow's colour'd line,—
See how its rose and amber clings
To the many hues of my radiant wings ;
Mine is the step that bids the earth
Give to the iris flower its birth,
And mine the golden cup to hide,
Where the last faint hue of the rainbow died.
Search the depths of an Indian mine,—
Where are the colours to match with mine ?

Chorus.   Dance we round, for the gale is bringing
Songs the summer rose is singing.

Third Fairy.   I float on the breath of a minstrel's lute,
Or the wandering sound￵ of a distant flute,
Linger I over the tones ᴜ..t swell
From the pink-veined chords of an ocean-shell ;
I love the skylark's morning hymn,
Or the nightingale heard at the twilight dim,
The echo, the fountain's melody,—
These, oh ! these are the spells for me !

Chorus.   Hail to the summer night of June ;
See ! yonder has risen our ladye moon.

Fourth Fairy.   My palace is in the coral cave
Set with spars by the ocean wave ;
Would ye have gems, then seek them there,—
There found I the pearls that bind my hair.

I and the wind together can roam
Over the green waves and their white foam,—
See, I have got this silver shell,
Mark how my breath will its smallness swell,
For the Nautilus is my boat
In which I over the waters float :
The moon is shining over the sea,—
Who is there will come sail with me?

Chorus of Fairies. Our noontide sleep is on leaf and
    flower,
Our revels are held in a moonlit hour,—
What is there sweet, what is there fair,
And we are not the dwellers there?
Dance we round, for the morning light
Will put us and our glow-worm lamps to flight !

L. E. L.

Chronicles of Fairyland.

NYMPHIDIA.

THE COURT OF FAIRY.

OLD Chaucer doth of Topas tell,
Mad Rablais of Pantagruel,
A later third of Dowsabel,
  With such poor trifles playing :
Others the like have labour'd at,
Some of this thing, and some of that,
And many of they know not what,
  But that they must be saying.

Another sort there be, that will
Be talking of the fairies still,
Nor never can they have their fill,
  As they were wedded to them :
No tales of them their thirst can slake,
So much delight therein they take,
And some strange thing they fain would make,
  Knew they the way to do them.

Then since no muse hath been so bold,
Or for the later, or the old,
Those elvish secrets to unfold,
  Which be from others' reading ;
My active muse to light shall bring
The court of that proud Fairy King,
And tell there of the revelling—
  Joy prosper my proceeding.

And thou, Nymphidia, gentle Fay,
Which, meeting me upon the way,
These secrets didst to me bewray,
    Which now I am in telling :
My pretty, light fantastic maid,
I here invoke to thee my aid,
That I may speak what thou hast said,
    In numbers smoothly swelling.

This palace standeth in the air,
By necromancy placèd there.
That it no tempests needs to fear,
    Which way soe'er it blow it :
And somewhat southward tow'rd the noon,
Whence lies a way up to the moon,
And thence the Fairy can as soon
    Pass to the earth below it.

The walls of spiders' legs are made,
Well morticed and finely laid,
He was the master of his trade,
    It curiously that builded :
The windows of the eyes of cats,
And for the roof, instead of flats,
Is cover'd with the skins of bats,
    With moonshine that are gilded.

Hence Oberon, him sport to make
(Their rest when weary mortals take,
And none but only Fairies wake),
    Descendeth for his pleasure ;
And Mab, his merry Queen, by night
Bestrides young folks that lie upright
(In elder times the Mare that hight),
    Which plagues them out of measure.

Hence shadows, seeming idle shapes,
Of little frisking elves and apes,
To earth do make their wanton scapes,
　　As hope of pastures hastes them :
Which maids think on the hearth they see,
When fires well-near consumèd be,
There dancing hayes by two and three,
　　Just as their fancy casts them.

These make our girls their flutt'ry rue,
By pinching them both black and blue,
And put a penny in their shoe,
　　The house for cleanly sweeping :
And in their courses make that round,
In meadows and in marshes found,
Of them so call'd the Fairy ground,
　　Of which they have the keeping.

These, when a child haps to be got,
Which after proves an idiot,
When folk perceive it thriveth not,
　　The fault therein to smother :
Some silly, doating, brainless calf,
That understands things by the half,
Say, that the Fairy left this aulf,
　　And took away the other

But listen, and I shall you tell
A chance in Fairy that befel,
Which certainly may please some well,
　　In love and arms delighting :
Of Oberon, that jealous grew
Of one of his own Fairy crew,
For well (he fear'd) his Queen that knew,
　　His love but ill requiting.

Pigwiggen was this Fairy Knight,
One wondrous gracious in the sight
Of fair Queen Mab, which day and night
    He amorously observed :
Which made King Oberon suspect
His service took too good effect,
His sauciness and often checkt,
    And could have wish'd him starved.

Pigwiggen gladly would commend
Some token to Queen Mab to send,
If sea or land him aught could lend,
    Were worthy of her wearing :
At length this lover doth devise
A bracelet made of emmets' eyes,
A thing he thought that she would prize,
    No whit her state impairing.

And to the Queen a letter writes,
Which he most curiously indites,
Conjuring her by all the rites
    Of love, she would be pleased
To meet him, her true servant, where
They might, without suspect or fear,
Themselves to one another clear,
    And have their poor hearts eased.

" At midnight the appointed hour,
And for the Queen a fitting bow'r,
(Quoth he) is that fair cowslip flow'r,
    On Hipcut-hill that groweth :
In all your train there's not a Fay,
That ever went to gather May,
But she hath made it in her way,
    The tallest there that groweth."

When by Tom Thum, a Fairy page,
He sent it, and doth him engage,
By promise of a mighty wage,
　　It secretly to carry ;
Which done, the Queen her maids doth call,
And bids them to be ready all,
She would go see her summer hall,
　　She could no longer tarry.

Her chariot ready strait is made,
Each thing therein is fitting laid,
That she by nothing might be stay'd,
　　For naught must be her letting :
Four nimble gnats the horses were,
Their harnesses of gossamere,
Fly Cranion, her charioteer,
　　Upon the coach-box getting.

Her chariot of a snail's fine shell,
Which for the colours did excel ;
The fair Queen Mab becoming well,
　　So lively was the limning :
The seat the soft woll of the bee,
The cover (gallantly to see)
The wing of a py'd butterflee,
　　I trow, was simple trimming.

The wheels composed of crickets' bones,
And daintily made for the nonce,
For fear of rattling on the stones,
　　With thistle-down they shod it :
For all her maidens much did fear,
If Oberon had chanc'd to hear,
That Mab his Queen should have been there,
　　He would not have abode it.

She mounts her chariot with a trice,
Nor would she stay for no advice,
Until her maids, that were so nice,
    To wait on her were fitted ;
But ran herself away alone ;
Which, when they heard, there was not one
But hasted after to be gone,
    As she had been diswitted.

Hop, and Mop, and Drop so clear,
Pip, and Trip, and Skip, that were
To Mab their sovereign dear,
    Her special maids of honour ;
Fib, and Tib, and Pinch, and Pin,
Tick, and Quick, and Jill, and Jin,
Tit, and Nit, and Wap, and Win,
    The train that wait upon her.

Upon a grasshopper they got,
And what with amble and with trot,
For hedge nor ditch they spared not,
    But after her they hie them.
A cobweb over them they throw,
To shield the wind if it should blow,
Themselves they wisely could bestow,
    Lest any should espy them.

But let us leave Queen Mab awhile,
Through many a gate, o'er many a stile,
That now had gotten by this wile,
    Her dear Pigwiggen kissing ;
And tell how Oberon doth fare,
Who grew as mad as any hare,
When he had sought each place with care,
    And found his Queen was missing.

By grisly Pluto he doth swear,
He rent his clothes, and tore his hair,
And as he runneth here and there,
    An acorn cup he getteth ;
Which soon he taketh by the stalk, -
About his head he lets it walk,
Nor doth he any creature baulk,
    But lays on all he meeteth.

The Tuscan poet doth advance,
The frantic Paladine of France,
And those more ancient do inhance
    Alcides in his fury,
And others Ajax Telamon :
But to this time there hath been none
So Bedlam as our Oberon,
    Of which I dare assure ye.

And first encount'ring with a wasp,
He in his arms the fly doth clasp,
As though his breath he forth would grasp,
    Him for Pigwiggen taking :
" Where is my wife, thou rogue ? (quoth he)
Pigwiggen, she is come to thee ;
Restore her, or thou dy'st by me."
    Whereat the poor wasp quaking,

Cries, " Oberon, great Fairy King,
Content thee, I am no such thing ;
I am a wasp, behold my sting ! "
    At which the Fairy started.
When soon away the wasp doth go,
Poor wretch was never frighted so,
He thought his wings were much too slow,
    O'erjoy'd they so were parted.

He next upon a glow-worm light
(You must suppose it now was night),
Which, for her hinder part was bright,
    He took to be a devil;
And furiously doth her assail
For carrying fire in her tail ;
He thrash'd her rough coat with his flail,
    The mad King fear'd no evil.

"Oh ! (quoth the glow-worm) hold thy hand,
Thou puissant King of Fairyland,
Thy mighty strokes who may withstand,
    Hold, or of life despair I ! "
Together then herself doth roll,
And tumbling down into a hole,
She seem'd as black as any coal,
    Which vext away the Fairy.

From thence he ran into a hive,
Amongst the bees he letteth drive,
And down their combs begins to rive,
    All likely to have spoiled :
Which with their wax his face besmear'd,
And with their honey daubed his beard ;
It would have made a man affear'd
    To see how he was moiled.

A new adventure him betides :
He met an ant, which he bestrides,
And post thereon away he rides
    Which with his haste doth stumble,
And came full over on her snout,
Her heels so threw the dirt about,
For she by no means could get out,
    But over him doth tumble.

And being in this piteous case,
And all beflurried head and face,
On runs he in this wild-goose chase,
    As here and there he rambles,
Half blind against a mole-hill hit,
And for a mountain taking it,
For all he was out of his wit,
    Yet to the top he scrambles.

And being gotten to the top,
Yet there himself he could not stop,
But down on th' other side doth chop,
    And to the foot came rumbling :
So that the grubs therein that bred,
Hearing such turmoil overhead,
Thought surely they had all been dead,
    So fearful was the jumbling.

And falling down into a lake,
Which him up to the neck doth take,
His fury it doth somewhat slake,
    He calleth for a ferry.
Where you may some recovery note,
What was his club he made his boat,
And in his oaken cup doth float,
    As safe as in a wherry.

Men talk of the adventures strange
Of Don Quishot, and of their change,
Through which he armèd oft did range,
    Of Sancha Panza's travel :
But should a man tell everything
Done by this frantic Fairy King,
And them in lofty numbers sing,
    It well his wits might gravel.

Scarce set on shore, but therewithal
He meeteth Puck, which most men call
Hobgoblin, and on him doth fall
    With words from phrenzy spoken:
"Hoh, hoh," quoth Hob, "God save thy grace,
Who drest thee in this piteous case?
He thus that spoil'd my sovereign's face,
    I would his neck were broken."

This Puck seems but a dreaming dolt,
Still walking like a ragged colt,
And oft out of a bush doth bolt,
    Of purpose to deceive us;
And leading us makes us to stray
Long winter nights out of the way,
And when we stroll in mire and clay,
    He doth with laughter leave us.

"Dear Puck," quoth he, "my wife is gone;
As e'er thou lov'st King Oberon,
Let everything but this alone,
    With vengeance and pursue her:
Bring her home alive or dead;
Or that vile thief Pigwiggen's head;
That villain hath defiled my bed,
    He to this folly drew her."

Quoth Puck, "My liege, I'll never lin,
But I will thorough thick and thin,
Until at length I bring her in,
    My dearest lord, ne'er doubt it."
Thorough brake, thorough brier,
Thorough mud, thorough mier,
Thorough water, thorough fier,
    And thus Puck goes about it.

This thing Nymphidia overheard,
That on this mad king had a guard,
Not doubting of a great reward,
    For first this bus'ness broaching :
And through the air away doth go
Swift as an arrow from the bow,
To let her sovereign Mab to know
    What peril was approaching.

The queen, bound with love's powerful charm,
Sate with Pigwiggen arm in arm ;
Her merry maids, that thought no harm,
    About the room were skipping :
A humble-bee their minstrel, play'd
Upon his haut-bois, every maid
Fit for this revel was array'd,
    The hornpipe neatly tripping.

In comes Nymphidia, and doth cry,
" My sovereign, for your safety fly,
For there is danger but too nigh,
    I posted to forewarn you :
The king hath sent Hobgoblin out,
To seek you all the fields about,
And of your safety you may doubt,
    If he but once discern you."

When like an uproar in a town,
Before them everything went down ;
Some tore a ruff, and some a gown,
    'Gainst one another jostling :
They flew about like chaff i' th' wind ;
For haste some left their masks behind,
Some could not stay their gloves to find ;
    There never was such bustling.

Forth ran they by a secret way,
Into a brake that near them lay,
Yet much they doubted there to stay,
    Lest Hob should hap to find them:
He had a sharp and piercing sight,
All one to him the day and night,
And therefore were resolv'd by flight
    To leave this place behind them.

At length one chanc'd to find a nut,
In th' end of which a hole was cut,
Which lay upon a hazel-root,
    There scatter'd by a squirrel,
Which out the kernel gotten had:
When quoth this Fay, "Dear queen, be glad,
Let Oberon be ne'er so mad,
    I'll set you safe from peril.

"Come all into this hut (quoth she),
Come closely in, be rul'd by me,
Each one may here a chuser be,
    For room ye need not wrestle,
Nor need ye be together heapt."
So one by one therein they crept,
And lying down, they soundly slept,
    As safe as in a castle.

Nymphidia, that this while doth watch,
Perceiv'd if Puck the queen should catch,
That he would be her over-match,
    Of which she well bethought her;
Found it must be some pow'rful charm,
The queen against him that must arm,
Or surely he would do her harm,
    For throughly he had sought her.

And list'ning if she aught could hear,
That her might hinder, or might fear;
But finding still the coast was clear,
    Nor creature had descry'd her:
Each circumstance and having scann'd,
She came thereby to understand,
Puck would be with them out of hand,
    When to her charms she hy'd her.

And first her fern seed doth bestow,
The kernel of the mistletoe;
And here and there as Puck should go,
    With terror to affright him,
She night-shade straws to work him ill,
Therewith her vervain and her dill,
That hind'reth witches of their will,
    Of purpose to despight him.

Then sprinkles she the juice of rue,
That groweth underneath the yew,
With wine drops of the midnight dew,
    From lunary distilling;
The wolewarp's brain mixt therewithal,
And with the same the pismire's gall:
For she in nothing short would fall,
    The Fairy was so willing.

Then thrice under a brier doth creep,
Which at both ends was rooted deep,
And over it three times did leap,
    Her magic much availing:
Then on Proserpina doth call,
And so upon her spell doth fall,
Which here to you repeat I shall,
    Not in one tittle failing.

" By the croaking of the frog ;
By the howling of the dog ;
By the crying of the hog
      Against the storm arising ;
By the evening curfew-bell ;
By the doleful dying knell ;
O let this my direful spell,
      Hob, hinder thy surprising.

" By the Mandrake's dreadful groans ;
By the Lubrican's sad moans ;
By the noise of dead men's boncs
      In charnel houses rattling ;
By the hissing of the snake,
The rustling of the fire-drake,
I charge thee this place forsake,
      Nor of Queen Mab be prattling.

" By the whirlwind's hollow sound,
By the thunder's dreadful stound,
Yells of spirits underground,
      I charge thee not to fear us :
By the screech-owl's dismal note,
By the black night-raven's throat,
I charge thee, Hob, to tear thy coat
      With thorns, if thou come near us.

Her spell thus spoke, she stept aside,
And in a chink herself doth hide,
To see thereof what would betide,
      For she doth only mind him :
When presently she Puck espies,
And well she markt his gloating eyes,
How under every leaf he pries,
      In seeking still to find them.

But once the circle got within,
The charms to work do straight begin,
And he was caught as in a gin :
    For as he thus was busy,
A pain he in his headpiece feels,
Against a stubbed tree he reels,
And up went poor Hobgoblin's heels ;
    Alas ! his brain was dizzy.

At length upon his feet he gets,
Hobgoblin fumes, Hobgoblin frets,
And as again he forward sets,
    And through the bushes scrambles,
A stump doth trip him in his pace,
Down comes poor Hob upon his face,
And lamentably tore his case
    Amongst the briars and brambles.

" Plague upon Queen Mab (quoth he),
And all her maids, where'er they be ;
I think the devil guided me,
    To seek her, so provoked."
When stumbling at a piece of wood,
He fell into a ditch of mud,
Where to the very chin he stood,
    In danger to be choaked.

Now worse than e'er he was before,
Poor Puck doth yell, poor Puck doth roar,
That waked Queen Mab, who doubted sore
    Some treason had been wrought her :
Until Nymphidia told the Queen
What she had done, what she had seen,
Who then had well-near crack'd her spleen
    With very extreme laughter.

But leave we Hob to clamber out,
Queen Mab and all her Fairy rout,
And come again to have a bout
    With Oberon yet madding :
And with Pigwiggen now distrought,
Who much was troubled in his thought,
That he so long the Queen had sought,
    And through the fields was gadding.

And as he runs, he still doth cry,
" King Oberon, I thee defy,
And dare thee here in arms to try,
    For my dear lady's honour :
In that she is a queen right good,
In whose defence I'll shed my blood,
And that thou in this jealous mood
    Hast laid this slander on her."

And quickly arms him for the field,
A little cockle-shell his shield,
Which he could very bravely wield,
    Yet could it not be pierced :
His spear a bent both stiff and strong,
And well near of two inches long ;
The pile was of a horse-fly's tongue,
    Whose sharpness nought reversed.

And puts him on a coat of mail,
Which was of a fishe's scale,
That when his foe should him assail,
    No point should be prevailing.
His rapier was a hornet's sting,
It was a very dangerous thing,
For if he chanc'd to hurt the king,
    It would be long in healing.

His helmet was a beetle's head,
Most horrible and full of dread,
That able was to strike one dead,
    Yet it did well become him :
And for a plume, a horse's hair,
Which being tossèd by the air,
Had force to strike his foe with fear,
    And turn his weapon from him.

Himself he on an earwig set,
Yet scarce he on his back could get,
So oft and high he did curvet,
    Ere he himself could settle :
He made him turn, and step, and bound,
To gallop, and to trot the round,
He scarce could stand on any ground,
    He was so full of mettle.

When soon he met with Tomalin,
One that a valiant knight had been,
And to great Oberon of kin :
    Quoth he, " Thou manly Fairy,
Tell Oberon I come prepar'd,
Then bid him stand upon his guard ;
This hand his baseness shall reward,
    Let him be ne'er so wary.

" Say to him thus, ' That I defy
His slanders and his infamy,
And as a mortal enemy
    Do publicly proclaim him :
Withal, that if I had mine own,
He should not wear the Fairy crown,
But with a vengeance should come down ;
    Not we a king should name him.' "

This Tomalin could not abide,
To hear his sovereign vilify'd ;
But to the Fairy court him hy'd,
     Full furiously he posted,
With ev'rything Pigwiggen said ;
How title to the crown he laid,
And in what arms he was array'd,
     And how himself he boasted.

'Twixt head and foot, from point to point,
He told the arming of each joint,
In every piece how neat and quaint ;
     For Tomalin could do it :
How fair he sat, how sure he rid ;
As of the courser he bestrid,
How manag'd, and how well he did.
     The king, which listen'd to it,

Quoth he, " Go, Tomalin, with speed,
Provide me arms, provide my steed,
And everything that I shall need,
     By thee I will be guided :
To strait account call thou thy wit,
See there be wanting not a whit,
In everything see thou me fit,
     Just as my foe's provided."

Soon flew this news through Fairy-land,
Which gave Queen Mab to understand
The combat that was then in hand
     Betwixt those men so mighty :
Which greatly she began to rue,
Perceiving that all Fairy knew,
The first occasion from her grew,
     Of these affairs so weighty.

Wherefore attended with her maids,
Through fogs, and mists, and damps she wades,
To Proserpine the Queen of Shades,
　　To treat, that it would please her
The cause into her hands to take,
For ancient love and friendship's sake,
And soon thereof an end to make,
　　Which of much care would ease her.

Awhile there let we Mab alone,
And come we to King Oberon,
Who arm'd to meet his foe is gone,
　　For proud Pigwiggen crying :
Who sought the Fairy King as fast,
And had so well his journies cast,
That he arrivèd at the last,
　　His puissant foe espying.

Stout Tomalin came with the King,
Tom Thumb doth on Pigwiggen bring,
That perfect were in ev'rything
　　To single fights belonging :
And therefore they themselves engage,
To see them exercise their rage,
With fair and comely equipage,
　　Not one the other wronging.

So like in arms these champions were,
As they had been a very pair,
So that a man could almost swear
　　That either had been either :
Their furious steeds began to neigh,
That they were heard a mighty way :
Their staves upon their rests they lay ;
　　Yet ere they flew together,

Their seconds minister an oath,
Which was indifferent to them both,
That on their knightly faith and troth,
　　No magic them supplied ;
And sought them that they had no charms,
Wherewith to work each other's harms,
But come with simple open arms,
　　To have their causes tried.

Together furiously they ran,
That to the ground came horse and man :
The blood out of their helmets span,
　　So sharp were their encounters :
And though they to the earth were thrown,
Yet quickly they regain'd their own ;
Such nimbleness was never shewn,
　　They were two gallant mounters.

When in a second course again,
They forward came with might and main,
Yet which had better of the twain,
　　The seconds could not judge yet :
Their shields were into pieces cleft,
Their helmets from their heads were 'reft,
And to defend them nothing left,
　　These champions would not budge yet.

Away from them their staves they threw,
Their cruel swords they quickly drew,
And freshly they the fight renew,
　　They every stroke redoubled :
Which made Proserpina take heed,
And make to them the greater speed,
For fear lest they too much should bleed,
　　Which wond'rously her troubled.

When to th' infernal Styx she goes,
She take the fogs from thence that rose,
And in a bag doth them enclose,
 When well she had them blended :
She hies her then to Lethe spring,
A bottle and thereof doth bring,
Wherewith she meant to work the thing
 Which only she intended.

Now Proserpine with Mab is gone
Unto the place where Oberon
And proud Pigwiggen, one to one,
 Both to be slain were likely :
And there themselves they closely hide,
Because they would not be espy'd ;
For Prosperpine meant to decide
 The matter very quickly.

And suddenly unties the poke,
Which out of it sent such a smoke,
As ready was them all to choke,
 So grievous was the pother :
So that the knights each other lost,
And stood as still as any post,
Tom Thumb nor Tomalin could boast
 Themselves of any other.

But when the mist 'gan somewhat cease,
Proserpina commandeth peace,
And that a while they should release
 Each other of their peril :
" Which here (quoth she) I do proclaim
To all, in dreadful Pluto's name,
That as ye will eschew his blame,
 You let me hear the quarrel.

"But here yourselves you must engage,
Somewhat to cool your spleenish rage,
Your grievous thirst and to assuage,
    That first you drink this liquor ;
Which shall your understandings clear,
As plainly shall to you appear,
Those things from me that you shall hear,
    Conceiving much the quicker."

This Lethe water, you must know,
The memory destroyeth so,
That of our weal, or of our woe,
    It all remembrance blotted,
Of it nor can you ever think :
For they no sooner took this drink,
But nought into their brains could sink,
    Of what had them besotted.

King Oberon forgotten had
That he for jealousy ran mad ;
But of his queen was wond'rous glad,
    And ask'd how they came thither.
Pigwiggen likewise doth forget
That he Queen Mab had ever met,
Or that they were so hard beset
    When they were found together.

Nor either of 'em both had thought
That e'er they had each other fought,
Much less that they a combat sought,
    But such a dream were loathing.
Tom Thumb had got a little sup,
And Tomalin scarce kiss'd the cup,
Yet had their brains so sure lockt up,
    That they remember'd nothing.

Queen Mab and her light maids the while
Amongst themselves do closely smile,
To see the king caught with this wile,
    With one another jesting :
And to the Fairy Court they went,
With mickle joy and merriment,
Which thing was done with good intent ;
    And thus I left them feasting.

                    MICHAEL DRAYTON.

PRINCE BRIGHTKIN.

SCENE : *A Forest in Fairyland.*

DAWN.

First Fairy.   FAIRIES and Elves !
            Shadows of night
            Pale and grow thin,
                Branches are stirr'd ;
            Rouse up yourselves ;
                Sing to the light,
            Fairies, begin,—
                Hark, there's a bird !

Second.   For dreams are now fading,
            Old thoughts in new morning ;
            Dull spectres and goblins
                To dungeon must fly.
            The starry night changeth,
            Its low stars are setting,
            Its lofty stars dwindle
            - And hide in the sky.

First.   Fairies, awake !
      Light on the hills !
      Blossom and grass
       Tremble with dew ;
      Gambols the snake,
       Merry bird shrills,
      Honey-bees pass,
       Morning is new.

Second.   Pure joy of the cloudlets,
      All rippled in crimson !
      Afar over world's edge
       The night-fear is roll'd ;
      O look how the Great One
      Uplifts himself kingly ;
      At once the wide morning
       Is flooded with gold !

First.   Fairies, arouse !
       Mix with your song
      Harplet and pipe,
       Thrilling and clear.
      Swarm on the boughs !
       Chant in a throng !
      Morning is ripe,
       Waiting to hear.

Second.   The merle and the skylark
      Will hush for our chorus,
      Quick wavelets of music,
       Begin them anon !
      Good-luck comes to all things
      That hear us and hearken,—
      Our myriads of voices
       Commingling in one.

General Chorus.   Golden, golden
Light unfolding,
Busily, merrily, work and play,
In flowery meadows,
And forest-shadows,
All the length of a summer day !
All the length of a summer day !

Sprightly, lightly,
Sing we rightly !
Moments brightly hurry away !
Fruit-tree blossoms,
And roses' bosoms—
Clear blue sky of a summer day !
Dear blue sky of a summer day !

Springlets, brooklets,
Greeny nooklets,
Hill and valley, and salt-sea spray !
Comrade rovers,
Fairy lovers,—
All the length of a summer day !
All the livelong summer day !

FORENOON.

Enter two Fairies (ROSLING *and* Another) *separately.*

First.   Greeting, brother !

Second.   Greet thee well !
Hast thou any news to tell?
How goes sunshine ?

First.   Flowers of noon
All their eyes will open soon,

While ours are closing.   What hast done
Since the rising of the sun?

Second.   Four wild snails I've taught their paces,
Pick'd the best ones for the races.
Thou?

First.   Where luscious dewdrops lurk,
I with fifty went to work,
Catching delicious wine that wets
The warm blue heart of violets;
Last moon it was hawthorn-flower,
Next moon 'twill be virgin's bower,
Moon by moon, the varied rose,—
To seal in flasks for winter mirth,
When frost and darkness wrap the earth.
Which wine delights you, fay?

Second.   All those;
But none is like the Wine of Rose.
With Wine of Rose,
In midst of snows
The sunny season flows and glows!

First.   Elf, thou lovest best, I think,
The time to sit in a cave and drink.

Second.   Is't not well to have good reason,
Thus, for loving every season?
White-rose wine
Is pure and fine,
But red-rose dew, dear tipple of mine!
The red flow'rs bud
In our summery blood,
And the nightingale sings in our brain like a
wood.

First.   Some who came a-gathering dew,
Tasting, sipping, fresh and new,
Tumbled down, an idle crew,
And there among the grass they lie,
Under a toadstool; any fly
May nip their foolish noses!

Second.   Soon
We shall hear the Call of Noon.

First.   They cannot stir to any tune.
No evening feast for them, be sure,
But far-off sentry on the moor.
Whence that sound of music?—hist!

Second.   Klingoling, chief lutanist,
A hundred song-birds in a ring
Is teaching all this morn to sing
Together featly, so to fill
The wedding-music,—loud and shrill,
Soft and sweet, and high and low,
Singled, mingled. He doth know
The art to make a hundred heard
Like one great surprising bird.

First.   Here comes Rosling! He'll report
All the doings of the Court.

Enter a Third Fairy.

Greeting, brothers!

First.   Greet thee well!
Hast thou any news to tell?
Our Princess dear, what shadow lies
Drooping on her blissful eyes?
Her suitors plague her?—is it so?

Third.   ·So in truth it is.   But, lo !
Who comes our way ?   Fairy, whence ?
Thou'rt a stranger.

Enter a Fourth Fairy.

No offence,
I trust, altho' my cap is blue,
While yours are green as any leaf.
Courteous fays !   No spy or thief
Is here, but one who longs to view
Your famous Forest ; chiefly there
Your Princess fair, the praised in song
Wheresoever fairies throng.
Oft you see her ?

Third.   Every day.

Fourth.   And is she lovely as they say ?

Third.   Thou hast not seen her ?   Dost thou think
Blue and golden, white and pink,
Could paint the magic of her face ?
All common beauty's highest place
Being under hers how far !—

Fourth.   How far ?

Third.   A glow-worm to the evening star.

First.   Scarce Klingoling could say so well !
'Tis true : so much she doth excel.
Come, fairy, to our feast to-night,
Two hours from sunset ; then you may
See the Forest-Realm's Delight.

Fourth.   But were it not presumptuous?

First.   Nay,
Thou art, I ween, a gentle fay,
And sure of welcome.

Fourth.   It is said
Her Highness shortly means to wed!

Third.   Next full moon, by fairy law,
She must marry, no escape,
Were it marsh-sprite, kobold, shape
Creeping from earth-hole with horn and claw!

Fourth.   And hath she now a suitor?   .

Third.   Three;
Bloatling, Rudling, Loftling; she
Loathes them all impartially.
The first is ugly, fat, and rich,
Grandson of a miser witch;
He sends her bossy peonies,
Fat as himself, to please her eyes,
And double poppies, mock flow'rs made
In clumsy gold, for brag display'd;
Ten of the broadest shoulder'd elves
To carry one must strain themselves.

First.   Aye! so I've seen them.

Second.   This is more
Than I ever heard before.

Third.   Field-marshal Rudling, soldier fay,
His beard a broom to sweep away
Opposition, with his frown
Biddeth common fairies, "Down!

Down on your knees !" and then his smile,
Our lovely Lady's heart to wile—
Soft as a rat-trap ! and his voice—
Angry jay makes no such noise
When bold marauders threat (as you,
Little Jinkling, sometimes do)
Her freckled eggs.

Fourth.   And Loftling?

Third.   True,
Prince Loftling's chin, so grand is he,
Is where another's nose would be ;
His proud backbone the wrong way bends
With nobleness.   He condescends
To come in state to our poor wood ;
And then 'tis always understood
We silence every prattling bird,
Nor must one grasshopper be heard ;
Which tasks our people ; she, meanwhile,
Our Lady, half dead with his vile
Ceremonial and precision,—
" Madam, with your august permission,
I have the honour to remark—
Ah hum ! ah haw !" from dawn to dark.

Fourth.   He will not win her !

Third.   No, no, no !
Dreary the wood if that were so,
Good stranger.   But enough, I ween,
Of gossip now.

Fourth.   Kind Caps o' Green,
I thank ye for your courtesies !
Brightkin's my name, my country lies

Round that blue peak your scout espies
From loftiest fir-tree on the skies
Of sunset.   So I take my leave
Till the drawing-on of eve.

First.   They call me Rosling, gentle fay.
Adieu ! forget not ; here I'll stay
To meet thee and to show the way.

All.   Adieu ! adieu ! till close of day.

THE NOON CALL.

Hear the call !
Fays, be still !
Noon is deep
On vale and hill.
Stir no sound
The Forest round !
Let all things hush
That fly or creep,—
Tree and bush,
Air and ground !
Hear the call !
Silence keep !
One and all
Hush and sleep !

NEAR SUNSET.

Two Fairies : ROSLING and JINKLING.

Ros.   Little Jinkling ! friend of mine !
Where dost lurk when fairies dine ?
At the banquet round and round
Searching, thee I never found.

Comest thou late ?   The feast is done ;
Slowly sinks the mighty sun.

Jink.   Nay, fay ! I was far away.
Over the tree-tops did I soar
Twenty leagues and twenty more.
Swift and high goes the dragon-fly,
    And steady the death's-head moth,
But the little bird with his beak awry
    Is a better saddle than both !
The lovely Lady of Elfin-Mere,
I had a message for her ear.

Ros.   Of state ?

Jink.   Of state : of import great,
I must not even to thee relate.

Ros   And is she fair ?

Jink.   Thrice fair is she ;
The pearly moon less delicately
Comes shining onward than this Lady
From her water-palace shady
Floats across the lucent lake,
And all her starry lilies make
Obeisance ; every water-sprite
Gazing after with delight,
Only wishing he might dare
Just to touch her streaming hair,
Meanwhile, crowds of fairies glide
Over, under, the crystal tide,
Some on swimming-birds astride,
Some with merry fishes at play,
Darting round her rippling way.

Ros.　　　.There was your banquet !

Jink.　　　　　　　　　There indeed,
Among the lily and the reed.
Wavy music, as we feasted,
Floating round us while we floated,
Soothed our pleasure and increased it ;
Mirth and jest more briskly glancing
Than the water-diamonds dancing
Down the lake where sunshine smote it.
Bright and gay !—might not stay !—
White the hand I kiss'd, O fay,
Leap'd on my bird, and sped away.
Hast any news to tell me?

Ros.　　　　　　　　　Much !
Never didst thou hear of such.

Jink.　　A fight with spiders ? —hornets ?—perils
Teasing owls, or chasing squirrels?
Or some little elf, poor soul,
Lost in-a winding rabbit-hole ?
Are the royal trees in danger?

Ros.　　Dost thou mind the Blue-cap Stranger,
Brightkin by his name, that we
Met ere noontide lullaby?

Jink.　　Came he to your Feast ?

Ros.　　　　　　　　　My friend,
Ask no more questions, but attend !
To the Feast he came with me,
The chamberlain most courteously
Placing us nigh the upper end.
Her Highness bow'd, and Brightkin gazed
On her face like one amazed,

While our Beauty's tender eyes
Rested with a sweet surprise
Upon the stranger-fairy : round
Went cates and wines, and Klingoling
With five new birds began to sing.
Then came a page on errand bound
To ask the stranger's name and realm :
" Brightkin of the Purple Helm,
From the Blue Mountain, fairy knight,
Flown thence to view the Forest,—might
It please her Highness." It did please.
So by and by we sat at ease
In shadowy bow'r, a favour'd ring,
Now talking, now with Klingoling
Join'd in a waft of harmony ;
And evermore there seem'd to be
'Twixt Brightkin and our Princess dear
A concord, more than string with string
And voice with voice rejoice one's ear.
And then *he* took the lute and sung,
  With modest grace and skilfully,
For tipt with honey seem'd his tongue ;
  At first a murmuring melody,
Like the far song of falling rills
Amid the foldings of the hills,
And ever nearer as it flew,
Shaping its figure, like a bird,
Till into Love's own form it grew
In every lovely note and word.
So sweet a song we never heard !
When, think what came ?

Jink.   I cannot think.

Ros.   A trumpet-blast that made us wink !
A hailstorm upon basking flowers !

Quick, sharp !—we started to our feet,
All save her Highness, mild and sweet,
Who said, "See who invades our bowers."

Jink.   Who was it, Rosling? quickly say !

Ros.   The King of the Blue Mountains, fay,
Seeking audience, without delay.
Fierce and frowning his look at first,
Like that uncivil trumpet-burst ;
But all his blackness alter'd soon,
Like clouds that melt upon the moon,
Before the gentle dignity
Of Her, Titania's child, whom we
Obey and love.

Jink.   Blest may she be !
But wherefore came the haughty King?

Ros.   Hear briefly an unusual thing.
His only Son, the prince and heir,
Kept with too strict and jealous care
Within the mountain boundaries,
To-day o'erleaps them all, and flies,
No elf knows whither : flies to-day—
The Lord of Gnomes being on his way,
Bringing to that mountain Court
His gem-clad heiress.   Here was sport !
Then couriers told the angry king
They saw the Prince on gray-dove's wing
Threading our forest ; and again
That he had join'd our Lady's train.
    "Madam ! is't so?"   "If this be so,
Great sir, I nothing know."   When lo !
Brightkin outspringing kneels.   "My son !"
Exclaims the king—"Ho ! seize and bind him !"

But swift her Highness—" Stay ! let none
Move hand or foot ! Great King, you find him
Here in the Forest-Realm, my rule
Whereof no fairy power may school,
Saving imperial Oberon.
Free came he hither, free shall go."
Then says the Prince, " If you command,
I leave you, Pride of Fairyland,
Else never ! " Briefly now to tell,
As briefly all these things befell,
'Twas clear as new-born star they loved ;
The Mountain-King their love approved ;
And all were happy.

Jink.   Where are they,
The King and Prince ?

Kos.   They fly away
On the sunset's latest ray.
To-morrow they will come again,
With a countless noble train :
And next full moon—the Wedding Feast !

Jink.   O joy ! the greatest and the least
Will join the revelry, and bring
A marriage-gift of some fine thing.
I know a present she will prize—
A team of spot-wing'd butterflies,
Right in flight, or else with ease
Winding through the tops of trees,
Or soaring in the summer sky.

Kos.   Well done, Jinkling !—Now, good-bye ;
Sleepy as a field-mouse I,
When paws and snout coil'd he doth lie.

Jink.   Hark to Klingoling's lute-playing !
On the poplar-spire a-swaying
Gently to the crescent moon.

Ros.   I cannot stay to hear the tune.

Jink.   I linger in the yellow light.

Ros.   And so, good-night !

Jink.   And so, good-night !

AFTER SUNSET.

Klingoling and a Faint Chorus.

Moon soon sets now ;
Elves cradled on the bough.
Day's fays drop asleep ;
Dreams through the forest creep.

Chorus.   When broadens the moonlight, we frolic and
jest ;
When darkles the forest, we sink into rest.

Shine, fine star above !
Love's come, happy love !
Haste, happy wedding-night,
Full moon, round and bright !

Chorus.   And not till her circle is low in the west
We'll cease from our dancing, or couch us to
rest !

Lute, mute fall thy strings !
Hush, every voice that sings !

Fade away, drowsy song,
Dim forest-aisles along !

Chorus.   Of all thy dear music a love-song is best !
Thou hushest—we're silent—we sink into rest.

WILLIAM ALLINGHAM.

THE CULPRIT FAY.

'TIS the middle watch of a summer's night—
The earth is dark but the heavens are bright ;
Nought is seen in the vault on high
But the stars, and the moon, and the cloudless sky,
And the flood which rolls its milky hue,
A river of light on the welkin blue.
The moon looks down on old Cronest,
She mellows the shades on his shaggy breast,
And seems his huge gray form to throw
In a silver cone on the wave below ;
His sides are broken by spots of shade,
By the walnut bough and the cedar made,
And through their clustering branches dark
Glimmers and dies the firefly's spark—
Like starry twinkles that momently break
Through the rifts of the gathering tempest's rack.

II.

The stars are on the moving stream,
    And fling, as its ripples gently flow,
A burnished length of wavy beam
    In an eel-like spiral line below ;

The winds are whist, and the owl is still,
  The bat in the shelvy rock is hid,
And nought is heard on the lonely hill
But the cricket's chirp, and the answer shrill
  Of the gauze-winged Katy-did ;
And the plaint of the wailing whip-poor-will,
  Who moans unseen, and ceaseless sings,
Ever a note of wail and wo,
  Till morning spreads her rosy wings,
And earth and sky in her glances glow.

III.

'Tis the hour of fairy ban and spell,
The wood-tick has kept the minutes well,
He has counted them all with click and stroke,
Deep in the heart of the mountain oak,
And he has awakened the sentry elve
  Who sleeps with him in the haunted tree,
To bid him ring the hour of twelve,
  And call the fays to their revelry ;
Twelve small strokes on his tinkling bell—
('Twas made of the white snail's pearly shell :)—
" Midnight comes, and all is well !
Hither, hither, wing your way !
'Tis the dawn of the fairy day."

IV.

They come from beds of lichen green,
They creep from the mullen's velvet screen ;
  Some on the backs of beetles fly
From the silver tops of moon-touched trees,
  Where they swung in their cobweb hammocks
    high,
And rocked about in the evening breeze ;

Some from the hum-bird's downy nest—
And, pillowed on plumes of his rainbow breast,
Had slumbered there till the charmed hour ;
Some had lain in the scoop of the rock,
With glittering ising-stars inlaid,
And some had opened the four-o'-clock,
And stole within its purple shade.
And now they throng the moonlight glade,
Above—below—on every side,
Their little minim forms arrayed
In the tricksey pomp of fairy pride !

V.

They come not now to print the lea,
In freak and dance around the tree,
Or at the mushroom board to sup,
And drink the dew from the buttercup ;—
A scene of sorrow waits them now,
For an Ouphe has broken his vestal vow ;
He has loved an earthly maid,
And left for her his woodland shade ;
He has lain upon her lip of dew,
And sunned him in her eye of blue,
Fanned her cheek with his wing of air,
Played in the ringlets of her hair,
And, nestling on her snowy breast,
Forgot the lily-king's behest.
For this the shadowy tribes of air
To the elfin court must haste away :—
And now they stand expectant there,
To hear the doom of the Culprit Fay.

VI.

The throne was reared upon the grass
Of spice-wood and of sassafras ;

On pillars of mottled tortoise-shell
   Hung the burnished canopy—
And o'er it gorgeous curtains fell
   Of the tulip's crimson drapery.
The monarch sat on his judgment-seat,
   On his brow the crown imperial shone,
The prisoner Fay was at his feet,
   And his peers were ranged around the throne.
He waved his sceptre in the air,
   He looked around and calmly spoke ;
His brow was grave and his eye severe,
   But his voice in a softened accent broke :—

VII.

" Fairy ! Fairy ! list and mark,
   Thou has broke thine elfin chain,
Thy flame-wood lamp is quenched and dark,
   And thy wings are dyed with a deadly stain—
Thou hast sullied thine elfin purity
   In the glance of a mortal maiden's eye ;
Thou hast scorned our dread decree,
And thou shouldst pay the forfeit high,
But well I know her sinless mind
Is pure as the angel forms above,
Gentle and meek, and chaste and kind,
Such as a spirit well might love ;
Fairy ! had she spot or taint,
Bitter had been thy punishment.
Tied to the hornet's shardy wings ;
Tossed on the pricks of nettles' stings ;
Or seven long ages doomed to dwell
With the lazy worm in the walnut-shell ;
Or every night to writhe and bleed
Beneath the tread of the centipede ;

Or bound in a cobweb dungeon dim,
Your jailer a spider huge and grim,
Amid the carrion bodies to lie,
Of the worm, and the bug, and the murdered fly :
These it had been your lot to bear,
Had a stain been found on the earthly fair.
Now list, and mark our mild decree—
Fairy, this your doom must be :—

VIII.

" Thou shalt seek the beach of sand
Where the water bounds the elfin land,
Thou shalt watch the oozy brine
Till the sturgeon leaps in the bright moonshine,
Then dart the glistening arch below,
And catch a drop from his glistening bow.
The water-sprites will wield their arms,
    And dash around, with roar and rave,
And vain are the woodland spirits' charms,
    They are the imps that rule the wave.
Yet trust thee in thy single might,
If thy heart be pure and thy spirit right,
Thou shalt win the warlock fight.

IX.

" If the spray-bead gem be won,
    The stain of thy wing is washed away,
But another errand must be done
    Ere thy crime be lost for aye ;
Thy flame-wood lamp is quenched and dark,
Thou must reillume its spark.
Mount thy steed and spur him high
To the heaven's blue canopy ;
And when thou seest a shooting star,
Follow it fast, and follow it far—

The last faint spark of its burning train
Shall light the elfin lamp again.
Thou hast heard our sentence, Fay ;
Hence ! to the water-side, away ! ''

X.

The goblin marked his monarch well ;
    He spake not, but he bowed him low,
Then plucked a crimson colen bell,
    And turned him round in act to go.
The way is long, he cannot fly,
    His soiled wing has lost its power,
And he winds adown the mountain high,
    For many a sore and weary hour.
Through dreary beds of tangled fern,
Through groves of nightshade dark and dern,
Over the grass and through the brake,
Where toils the ant and sleeps the snake ;
    Now o'er the violet's azure flush
He skips along in lightsome mood :
    And now he thrids the bramble-bush,
Till its points are dyed in fairy blood.
He has leaped the bog, he has pierced the briar,
He has swam the brook, and waded the mire,
Till his spirits sank, and his limbs grew weak,
And the red waxed fainter in his cheek.
He had fallen to the ground outright,
    For rugged and dim was his onward track,
But there came a spotted toad in sight,
    And he laughed as he jumped upon her back ;
He bridled her mouth with a silkweed twist,
    He lashed her sides with an osier thong ;
And now through evening's dewy mist
    With leap and spring they bound along,

Till the mountain's magic verge is past,
And the beach of sand is reached at last.

XI.

Soft and pale is the moony beam,
Moveless still the glassy stream,
The wave is clear, the beach is bright
    With snowy shells and sparkling stones;
The shore-surge comes in ripples light,
    In murmurings faint and distant moans;
And ever afar in the silence deep
Is heard the splash of the sturgeon's leap,
And the bend of his graceful bow is seen—
A glittering arch of silver sheen,
Spanning the wave of burnished blue,
And dripping with gems of the river dew.

XII.

The elfin cast a glance around,
    As he lighted down from his courser toad,
Then round his breast his wings he wound,
    And close to the river's brink he strode;
He sprang on a rock, he breathed a prayer,
    Above his head his arms he threw,
Then tossed a tiny curve in air,
    And headlong plunged in the waters blue.

XIII.

Up sprung the spirits of the waves,
From sea-silk beds in their coral caves,
With snail-plate armour snatched in haste,
They speed their way through the liquid waste;
Some are rapidly borne along
On the mailed shrimp or the prickly prong,

Some on the blood-red leeches glide,
Some on the stony star-fish ride,
Some on the back of the lancing squab,
Some on the sideling soldier-crab ;
And some on the jellied quarl, that flings
At once a thousand streamy stings ;
They cut the wave with the living oar,
And hurry on to the moonlight shore,
To guard their realms and chase away
The footsteps of the invading Fay.

XIV.

Fearlessly he skims along,
His hope is high, and his limbs are strong,
He spreads his arms like the swallow's wing,
And throws his feet with a frog-like fling ;
His locks of gold on the water shine,
    At his breast the tiny foam-beds rise,
His back gleams bright above the brine,
    And the wake-line foam behind him lies.
But the water-sprites are gathering near
    To check his course along the tide ;
Their warriors come in swift career
    And hem him round on every side ;
On his thigh the leech has fixed his hold,
The quarl's long arms are round him rolled,
The prickly prong has pierced his skin,
And the squab has thrown his javelin,
The gritty star has rubbed him raw,
And the crab has struck with his giant claw ;
He howls with rage and he shrieks with pain,
He strikes around, but his blows are vain ;
Hopeless is the unequal fight,
Fairy ! nought is left but flight.

XV.

He turned him round and fled amain
With hurry and dash to the beach again,
He twisted over from side to side,
And laid his cheek to the cleaving tide.
The strokes of his plunging arms are fleet,
And with all his might he flings his feet,
But the water-sprites are round him still,
To cross his path and work him ill,
They bade the wave before him rise ;
They flung the sea-fire in his eyes,
And they stunned his ears with the scallop stroke,
With the porpoise heave and the drum-fish croak.
Oh ! but a weary wight was he
When he reached the foot of the dogwood tree
—Gashed and wounded, and stiff and sore,
He laid him down on the sandy shore ;
He blessed the force of the charmed line,
    And he banned the water-goblins' spite,
For he saw around in the sweet moonshine
Their little wee faces above the brine,
Giggling and laughing with all their might
At the piteous hap of the fairy wight.

XVI.

Soon he gathered the balsam dew
    From the sorrel-leaf and the henbane bud ;
Over each wound the balm he drew,
    And with cobweb lint he stanched the blood.
The mild west wind was soft and low,
It cooled the heat of his burning brow,
And he felt new life in his sinews shoot,
As he drank the juice of the cal'mus root ;
And now he treads the fatal shore
As fresh and vigorous as before.

XVII.

Wrapped in musing stands the sprite :
'Tis the middle wane of night,
  His task is hard, his way is far,
But he must do his errand right
  Ere dawning mounts her beamy car,
And rolls her chariot wheels of light ;
And vain are the spells of fairy-land,
He must work with a human hand.

XVIII.

He cast a saddened look around,
  But he felt new joy his bosom swell,
When, glittering on the shadowed ground,
  He saw a purple mussel shell ;
Thither he ran, and he bent him low,
He heaved at the stern, and he heaved at the bow,
And he pushed her over the yielding sand,
Till he came to the verge of the haunted land.
She was as lovely a pleasure-boat
  As ever fairy had paddled in,
For she glowed with purple paint without,
  And shone with silver pearl within ;
A sculler's notch in the stern he made,
An oar he shaped of the bootle-blade ;
Then sprung to his seat with a lightsome leap,
And launched afar on the calm blue deep.

XIX.

The imps of the river yell and rave ;
They had no power above the wave,
  But they heaved the billow before the prow,
And they dashed the surge against her side,
And they struck her keel with jerk and blow,
  Till the gunwale bent to the rocking tide.

She wimpled about in the pale moonbeam,
Like a feather that floats on a wind-tossed stream ;
And momently athwart her track
The quarl upreared his island back,
And the fluttering scallop behind would float,
And spatter the water about the boat ;
But he bailed her out with his colen-bell,
    And he kept her trimmed with a wary tread,
While on every side like lightning fell
    The heavy strokes of his bootle-blade.

XX.

Onward still he held his way,
Till he came where the column of moonshine lay,
And saw beneath the surface dim
The brown-backed sturgeon slowly swim :
Around him were the goblin train—
But he sculled with all his might and main,
And followed wherever the sturgeon led,
Till he saw him upward point his head ;
Then he dropped his paddle blade,
And held his colen-goblet up
To catch the drop in its crimson cup.

XXI.

With sweeping tail and quivering fin,
    Through the wave the sturgeon flew,
And, like the heaven-shot javelin,
    He sprang above the waters blue.
Instant as the star-fall light,
    He plunged him in the deep again,
But left an arch of silver bright,
    The rainbow of the moony main.

It was a strange and lovely sight
  To see the puny goblin there ;
He seemed an angel form of light,
  With azure wing and sunny hair,
Throned on a cloud of purple fair,
Circled with blue and edged with white,
And sitting at the fall of even
Beneath the bow of summer heaven.

XXII.

A moment, and its lustre fell,
  But ere it met the billow blue,
He caught within his crimson bell,
  A droplet of its sparkling dew—
Joy to thee, Fay ! thy task is done,
Thy wings are pure, for the gem is won—
Cheerily ply the dripping oar,
And haste away to the elfin shore.

XXIII.

He turns, and lo ! on either side
The ripples on his path divide ;
And the track o'er which his boat must pass
Is smooth as a sheet of polished glass.
Around, their limbs the sea-nymphs lave,
  With snowy arms half swelling out,
While on the glossed and gleamy wave
  Their sea-green ringlets loosely float ;
They swim around with smile and song ;
  They press the bark with pearly hand,
And gently urge her course along,
  Toward the beach of speckled sand ;
  And, as he lightly leaped to land,
They bade adieu with nod and bow,

Then gaily kissed each little hand,
And dropped in the crystal deeps below.

XXIV.

A moment stayed the fairy there ;
He kissed the beach and breathed a prayer,
Then spread his wings of gilded blue,
And on to the elfin court he flew ;
As ever ye saw a bubble rise,
And shine with a thousand changing dyes,
Till lessening far through ether driven,
It mingles with the hues of heaven ;
As, at the glimpse of morning pale,
The lance-fly spreads his silken sail,
And gleams with blending soft and bright,
Till lost in the shades of fading night ;
So rose from earth the lovely Fay—
So vanished, far in heaven away !

. . . .

Up, Fairy ! quit thy chick-weed bower,
The cricket has called the second hour,
Twice again, and the lark will rise
To kiss the streaking of the skies—
Up ! thy charmed armour don,
Thou'lt need it ere the night be gone.

XXV.

He put his acorn-helmet on ;
It was plumed of the silk of the thistle-down ;
The corslet-plate that guarded his breast
Was once the wild-bees' golden vest ;
His cloak of a thousand mingled dyes,
Was formed of the wings of butterflies ;
His shield was the shell of a lady-bug queen,
Studs of gold on a ground of green ;

And the quivering lance which he brandished
  bright,
Was the sting of a wasp he had slain in fight.
Swift he bestrode his firefly steed ;
  He bared his blade of the bent grass blue ;
He drove his spurs of the cockle-seed,
  And away like a glance of thought he flew,
To skim the heavens and follow far
The fiery trail of the rocket-star.

XXVI.

The moth-fly, as he shot in air,
Crept under the leaf, and hid her there ;
The katy-did forgot its lay,
The prowling gnat fled fast away,
The fell moscheto checked his drone
And folded his wings till the Fay was gone,
And the wily beetle dropped his head,
And fell on the ground as if he were dead ;
They crouched them close in the darksome shade,
  They quaked all o'er with awe and fear,
For they had felt the blue-bent blade,
  And writhed at the prick of the elfin spear ;
Many a time on a summer's night,
When the sky was clear and the moon was bright,
They had been roused from the haunted ground,
By the yelp and bay of the fairy hound ;
They had heard the tiny bugle-horn,
They had heard the twang of the maize-silk string,
When the vine-twig boughs were tightly drawn,
And the nettle shaft through air was borne,
Feathered with down of the hum-bird's wing.
And now they deemed the courier ouphe,
  Some hunter sprite of the elfin ground ;
And they watched till they saw him mount the roof
  That canopies the world around ;

Then glad they left their covert lair,
And freaked about in the midnight air.

XXVII.

Up to the vaulted firmament
His path the firefly courser bent,
And at every gallop on the wind,
He flung a glittering spark behind;
He flies like a feather in the blast
Till the first light cloud in heaven is past,
  But the shapes of air have begun their work,
And a drizzly mist is round him cast,
  He cannot see through the mantle murk,
He shivers with cold, but he urges fast,
  Through storm and darkness, sleet, and shade,
He lashes his steed, and spurs amain,
For shadowy hands have twitched the rein,
  And flame-shot tongues around him played,
And near him many a fiendish eye
Glared with a fell malignity,
And yells of rage, and shrieks of fear,
Came screaming on his startled ear.
His wings are wet around his breast,
The plume hangs dripping from his crest,
His eyes are blurred with the lightning's glare,
And his ears are stunned with the thunder's blare,
But he gave a shout, and his blade he drew,
  He thrust before, and he struck behind,
Till he pierced their cloudy bodies through,
  And gashed their shadowy limbs of wind ;
Howling the misty spectres flew,
  They rend the air with frightful cries,
For he has gained the welkin blue,
  And the land of clouds beneath him lies.

XXIX.

Up to the cope careering swift
  In breathless motion fast,
Fleet as the swallow cuts the drift,
  Or the sea-roc rides the blast,
The sapphire sheet of eve is shot,
  The sphered moon is past,
The earth but seems a tiny blot
  On a sheet of azure cast.
O ! it was sweet in the clear moonlight,
  To tread the starry plain of even,
To meet the thousand eyes of night,
  And feel the cooling breath of heaven ;
But the Elfin made no stop or stay
Till he came to the bank of the milky-way,
Then he checked his courser's foot,
And watched for the glimpse of the planet-shoot.

XXX.

Sudden along the snowy tide
  That swelled to meet their footsteps' fall,
The sylphs of heaven were seen to glide,
  Attired in sunset's crimson pall ;
Around the Fay they weave the dance,
  They skip before him on the plain,
And one has taken his wasp-sting lance,
  And one upholds his bridle-rein ;
With warblings wild they lead him on
  To where through clouds of amber seen,
Studded with tsars, resplendent shone
  The palace of the sylphid queen.
Its spiral columns gleaming bright
Were streamers of the northern light ;
Its curtains' light and lovely flush
Was of the morning's rosy blush,

And the ceiling fair that rose aboon
The white and feathery fleece of noon.

XXXI.

But oh ! how fair the shape that lay
   Beneath a rainbow bending bright,
She seemed to the entranced Fay
   The loveliest of the forms of light ;
Her mantle was the purple rolled
   At twilight in the west afar ;
'Twas tied with threads of dawning gold,
   And buttoned with a sparkling star.
Her face was like the lily roon
   That veils the vestal planet's hue ;
Her eyes two beamlets from the moon,
   Set floating in the welkin blue.
Her hair is like the sunny beam,
And the diamond gems which round it gleam,
Are the pure drops of dewy even
That ne'er have left their native heaven.

XXXII.

She raised her eyes to the wondering sprite,
   And they leaped with smiles, for well I ween
Never before in the bowers of light
   Had the form of an earthly Fay been seen.
Long she looked in his tiny face ;
   Long with his butterfly cloak she played ;
She smoothed his wings of azure lace,
   And handled the tassel of his blade ;
And as he told in accents low
The story of his love and woe,
She felt new pains in her bosom rise,
And the tear-drop started in her eyes.

And " O, sweet spirit of earth," she cried,
   Return no more to your woodland height,
But ever here with me abide
   In the land of everlasting light !
Within the fleecy drift we'll lie,
   We'll hang upon the rainbow's rim,
And all the jewels of the sky
Around thy brow shall brightly beam !
And thou shalt bathe thee in the stream
   That rolls its whitening foam aboon,
And ride upon the lightning's gleam,
   And dance upon the orbéd moon !
We'll sit within the Pleiad ring,
   We'll rest on Orion's starry belt,
And I will bid my sylphs to sing
   The song that makes the dew-mist melt ;
Their harps are of the umber shade
   That hides the blush of waking day,
And every gleamy string is made
   Of silvery moonshine's lengthened ray ;
And thou shalt pillow on my breast
   While heavenly breathings float around,
And, with the sylphs of ether blest,
   Forget the joys of fairy ground."

XXXIII.

She was lovely and fair to see,
And the Elfin's heart beat fitfully ;
But lovelier far, and still more fair,
The earthly form imprinted there ;
Nought he saw in the heavens above
Was half so dear as his mortal love,
For he thought upon her looks so meek,
And he thought of the light flush on her cheek ;

Never again might he bask and lie
On that sweet cheek and moonlight eye,
But in his dreams her form to see,
To clasp her in his revery,
To think upon his virgin bride
Was worth all heaven and earth beside.

XXXIV.

"Lady," he cried, ." I have sworn to-night
On the word of a fairy knight,
To do my sentence-task aright;
My honour scarce is free from stain,
I may not soil its snows again;
Betide me weal, betide me woe,
Its mandate must be answered now."
Her bosom heaved with many a sigh,
The tear was in her drooping eye;
    But she led him to the palace gate,
And called the sylphs who hovered there,
    And bade them fly and bring him straight
Of clouds condensed a sable car.
With charm and spell she blessed it there,
From all the fields of upper air;
Then round him cast the shadowy shroud,
And tied his steed behind the cloud;
And pressed his hand as she bade him fly
Far to the verge of the northern sky,
For by its wan and wavering light
There was a star would fall to-night.

XXXV.

Borne afar on the wings of the blast,
Northward away, he speeds him fast,
And his courser follows the cloudy wain
Till the hoof strokes fall like pattering rain.

The clouds roll backward as he flies,
Each flickering star behind him lies,
And he has reached the northern plain,
And backed his firefly steed again,
Ready to follow in its flight
The streaming of the rocket-light.

XXXVI.

The star is yet in the vault of heaven,
 But it rocks in the summer gale;
And now 'tis fitful and uneven,
 And now 'tis deadly pale;
And now 'tis wrapped in sulphur smoke,
 And quenchéd is its rayless beam,
And now with a rattling thunder-stroke
 It bursts in flash and flame.
As swift as the glance of the arrowy lance
 That the storm-spirit flings from high,
The star-shot flew o'er the welkin blue,
 As it fell from the sheeted sky.
As swift as the wind in its trail behind
 The elfin gallops along,
The fiends of the cloud are bellowing loud,
 But the sylphid charm is strong;
He gallops unhurt in the shower of fire,
 While the cloud-fiends fly from the blaze;
He watches each flake till its sparks expire,
 And rides in the light of its rays.
But he drove his steed to the lightning's speed,
 And caught a glimmering spark;
Then wheeled around to the fairy ground,
 And sped through the midnight dark.

. . . . .

Ouphe and goblin! imp and sprite!
 Elf of eve! and starry Fay!

Ye that love the moon's soft light,
  Hither—hither wend your way;
Twine ye in a jocund ring,
  Sing and trip it merrily,
Hand to hand, and wing to wing,
  Round the wild witch-hazel tree.

Hail the wanderer again,
  With dance and song, and lute and lyre,
Pure his wing and strong his chain,
  And doubly bright his fairy fire.
Twine ye in an airy round,
  Brush the dew and print the lea;
Skip and gambol, hop and bound,
  Round the wild witch-hazel tree.

The beetle guards our holy ground,
  He flies about this haunted place,
And if mortal there be found,
  He hums in his ears and flaps his face:
The leaf-harp sounds our roundelay,
  The owlet's eyes our lanterns be;
Thus we sing, and dance, and play,
  Round the wild witch-hazel tree.

But hark! from tower on tree-top high,
  The sentry elf his call has made,
A streak is in the Eastern sky,
  Shapes of moonlight! flit and fade!
The hill-tops gleam in morning's spring,
The skylark shakes his dappled wing,
The day-glimpse glimmers on the lawn,
The cock has crowed, and the Fays are gone.

J. RODMAN DRAKE.

Travels in Fairyland.

442

THOMAS THE RHYMER.

PART FIRST—ANCIENT.

TRUE THOMAS lay on Huntlie bank
   A ferlie he spied wi' his ee ;
And there he saw a ladye bright
   Come riding doun by the Eildon Tree.

Her shirt was o' the grass-green silk,
   Her mantle o' the velvet fine ;
At ilka tett o' her horse's mane
   Hung fifty siller bells and nine.

True Thomas, he pulled aff his cap,
   And louted low down to his knee,
" All hail, thou mighty Queen of Heaven !
   For thy peer on earth I never did see."

" O no, O no, Thomas," she said,
   " That name does not belang to me ;
I am but the Queen of fair Elfland,
   That am hither come to visit thee.

" Harp and carp, Thomas," she said ;
   " Harp and carp along wi' me ;
And if ye dare to kiss my lips,
   Sure of your bodie I will be."—

" Betide me weal, betide me wo,
   That weird shall never daunton me."
Syne he has kiss'd her rosy lips,
   All underneath the Eildon Tree.

" Now, ye maun go wi' me," she said ;
    " True Thomas, ye maun go wi' me ;
And ye maun serve me seven years,
    Thro' weal or wo as may chance to be."

She mounted on her milk-white steed ;
    She's ta'en true Thomas up behind :
And aye, whene'er her bridle rung,
    The steed flew swifter than the wind.

O they rade on, and farther on ;
    The steed gaed swifter than the wind ;
Until they reach'd a desert wide,
    And living land was left behind.

" Light down, light down, now, true Thomas,
    And lean your head upon my knee ;
Abide and rest a little space,
    And I will show you ferlies three.

" O see ye not yon narrow road,
    So thick beset with thorns and briers ?
That is the path of righteousness,
    Though after it but few inquires.

" And see ye not that braid braid road,
    That lies across that lily leven ?
That is the path of wickedness,
    Though some call it the road to heaven.

" And see not ye that bonny road,
    That winds about that fernie brae ?
That is the road to fair Elfland,
    Where thou and I this night maun gae.

" But, Thomas, ye maun hold your tongue,
  Whatever ye may hear or see ;
For if you speak word in Elflyn land,
  Y'll ne'er get back to your ain countrie."

O they rade on, and farther on,
  And they waded through rivers aboon the knee,
And they saw neither sun nor moon,
  But they heard the roaring of the sea.

It was mirk mirk night, and there was nae stern light,
  And they waded through red blude to the knee ;
For a' the blude that's shed on earth
  Rins through the springs o' that countrie.

Syne they came on to a garden green,
  And she pu'd an apple frae a tree —
" Take this for thy wages, true Thomas,
  It will give thee the tongue that can never lie."

" My tongue is mine ain," true Thomas said ;
  A gudely gift ye wad gie to me !
I neither dought to buy nor sell,
  At fair or tryst where I may be.

" I dought neither speak to prince or peer,
  Nor ask of grace from fair ladye—"
" Now hold thy peace !" the lady said,
  " For as I say, so must it be."—

He has gotten a coat of the even cloth,
  And a pair of shoes of velvet green ;
And till seven years were gane and past,
  True Thomas on earth was never seen.

PART THE SECOND.

When seven years were come and gane,
 The sun blinked fair on pool and stream ;
And Thomas lay on Huntlie bank -
 Like one awakened from a dream.

He heard the trampling of a steed,
 He saw the flash of armour flee,
And he beheld a gallant knight,
 Come riding doun by the Eildon-tree.

He was a stalwart knight, and strong ;
 Of giant make he 'pear'd to be :
He stirr'd his horse, as he were wode,
 Wi' guilded spurs, of fashion free.

Says—" Well met, well met, true Thomas !
 Some uncouth ferlies show to me."
Says—" Christ thee save, Corspatrick brave !
 Thrice welcome, good Dunbar, to me !"

" Light down, light down, Corspatrick brave,
 And I will show thee curses three,
Shall gar fair Scotland greet and grane,
 And change the green to the black livery.

" A storm shall roar this very hour,
 From Ross's hills to Solway sea—"
" Ye lied, ye lied, ye warlock hoar !
 For the sun shines sweet on fauld and lea."---

He put his hand on the Earlie's head ;
 He showed him a rock beside the sea,
Where a king lay stiff beneath his steed,
 And steel-dight nobles wiped their ee.

" The neist curse lights on Branxton hills :
 By Flodden's high and heathery side,
Shall wave a banner red as blude,
 And chieftains hung wi' meikle pride.

" A Scottish King shall come full keen,
 The ruddy lion beareth he ;
A feather'd arrow sharp, I ween,
 Shall make him wink and warre to see.

" When he is bloody, and all to bledde,
 Thus to his men he still shall say—
' For God's sake, turn ye back again,
 And give yon southern folk a fray !
Why should I lose the right is mine?
 My doom is not to die this day.'

" Yet turn ye to the eastern hand,
 And wo and wonder ye shall see ;
How forty thousand spearman stand,
 Where yon rank river meets the sea.

" There shall the lion lose the gylte,
 And the libbards bear it clean away ;
At Pinkyn Cleuch there shall be split
 Much gentil bluid that day."—

" Enough, enough, of curse and ban ;
 Some blessings show thou now to me,
Or, by the faith o' my bodie," Corspatrick said,
 " Ye shall rue the day ye e'er saw me ! "

" The first of blessings I shall thee show,
 Is by a burn that's call'd of bread ;
Where Saxon men shall tyne the bow,
 And find their arrows lack the head.

" Beside that brigg, out ower that burn,
　　Where the water bickereth bright and sheen,
Shall many a falling courser spurn,
　　And knights shall die in battle keen.

" Beside a headless cross of stone,
　　The libbards there shall lose the gree ;
The raven shall come, the erne shall go,
　　And drink the Saxon bluid sae free.
The cross of stone they shall not know,
　　So thick the corses there shall be."

" But tell me now," said brave Dunbar,
　　" True Thomas, tell now unto me,
What man shall rule the isle Britain,
　　Even from the north to the southern sea ?"

" A French Queen shall bear the son,
　　Shall rule all Britain to the sea ;
He of the Bruce's blood shall come,
　　As near as in the ninth degree.

" The waters worship shall his race ;
　　Likewise the waves of the farthest sea ;
For they shall ride over ocean wide,
　　With hempen bridles and horse of tree."

PART THE THIRD.—MODERN.

By Walter Scott.

When seven years more were come and gone,
　　Was war through Scotland spread,
And Ruberslaw show'd high Dunyon
　　His beacon blazing red.

Then all by bonny Coldingknow,
    Pitch'd palliounes took their room,
And crested helms, and spears a-rowe,
    Glanced gaily through the broom.

The Leader, rolling to the Tweed,
    Resounds the ensenzie ;
They roused the deer from Caddenhead,
    To distant Torwoodlee.

The feast was spread in Ercildoune,
    In Learmont's high and ancient hall :
And there were knights of great renown,
    And ladies, laced in pall.

Nor lacked they, while they sat at dine,
    The music nor the tale,
Nor goblets of the blood-red wine,
    Nor mantling quaighs of ale.

True Thomas rose, with harp in hand,
    When as the feast was done :
(In minstrel strife, in Fairy Land,
    The elfin harp he won.)

Hush'd were the throng, both limb and tongue,
    And harpers for envy pale ;
And armed lords lean'd on their swords,
    And hearken'd to the tale.

In numbers high, the witching tale
    The prophet pour'd along ;
No after bard might e'er avail
    Those numbers to prolong.

Yet fragments of the lofty strain
　Float down the tide of years,
As buoyant on the stormy main
　A parted wreck appears.

He sung King Arthur's Table Round ;
　The Warrior of the Lake :
How courteous Gawaine met the wound,
　And bled for ladies' sake.

But chief, in gentle Tristrem's praise,
　The notes melodious swell ;
Was none excell'd in Arthur's days,
　The Knight of Lionelle.

For Marke, his cowardly uncle's right,
　A venom'd wound he bore ;
When fierce Morholde he slew in fight,
　Upon the Irish shore.

No art the poison might withstand ;
　No medicine could be found,
Till lovely Isolde's lily hand
　Had probed the rankling wound.

With gentle hand and soothing tongue
　She bore the leech's part ;
And while she o'er his sick-bed hung,
　He paid her with his heart.

O fatal was the gift, I ween !
　For, doom'd in evil tide,
The maid must be rude Cornwall's queen,
　His cowardly uncle's bride.

Their loves, their woes, the gifted bard
   In fairy tissue wove;
Where lords, and knights, and ladies bright,
   In gay confusion strove.

The Garde Joyeuse, amid the tale,
   High-rear'd its glittering head;
And Avalon's enchanted vale
   In all its wonders spread.

Brangwain was there, and Segramore,
   And fiend-born Merlin's gramarye;
Of that famed wizard's mighty lore,
   O who could sing but he?

Through many a maze the winning song
   In changeful passion led,
Till bent at length the listening throng
   O'er Tristrem's dying bed.

His ancient wounds their scars expand,
   With agony his heart is wrung:
O where is Isolde's lily hand,
   And where her soothing tongue?

She comes! she comes!—like flash of flame
   Can lovers' footsteps fly;
She comes! She comes!—she only came
   To see her Tristrem die.

She saw him die; her latest sigh
   Joined in a kiss his parting breath;
The gentlest pair, that Britain bare,
   United are in death.

Then paused the harp : its lingering sound
    Died slowly on the ear ;
The silent guests still bent around,
    For still they seem'd to hear.

Then wo broke forth in murmurs weak :
    Nor ladies heaved alone the sigh :
But, half ashamed, the rugged cheek
    Did many a gauntlet dry.

On Leader's stream, and Learmont's tower,
    The mists of evening close ;
In camp, in castle, or in bower,
    Each warrior sought repose.

Lord Douglas, in his lofty tent,
    Dream'd o'er the woful tale :
When footsteps light across the bent
    The warrior's ears assail.

He starts, he wakes ;—" What, Richard, ho !
    Arise, my page, arise !
What venturous wight, at dead of night,
    Dare step where Douglas lies ! "—

Then forth they rush'd ; by Leader's tide,
    A selcouth sight they see—
A hart and hind pace side by side,
    As white as snow on Fairnalie.

Beneath the moon, with gesture proud,
    They stately move and slow ;
Nor scare they at the gathering crowd,
    Who marvel as they go.

To Learmont's tower a message sped,
    As fast as page might run ;
And Thomas started from his bed,
    And soon his clothes did on.

First he woxe pale, and then woxe red ;
    Never a word he spake but three ;—
" My sand is run ; my thread is spun ;
    This sign regardeth me."

The elfin harp his neck around,
    In minstrel guise, he hung :
And on the wind, in doleful sound,
    Its dying accents rung.

Then forth he went ; yet turn'd him oft
    To view his ancient hall :
On the gray tower, in lustre soft,
    The autumn moonbeams fall ;

And Leader's waves, like silver sheen,
    Danced shimmering in the ray ;
In deepening mass, at distance seen,
    Broad Soltra's mountains lay.

" Farewell, my father's ancient tower !
    A long farewell," said he :
" The scene of pleasure, pomp, or power,
    Thou never more shalt be.

" To Learmont's name no foot of earth
    Shall here again belong,
And on thy hospitable hearth
    The hare shall leave her young.

" Adieu ! adieu !" again he cried,
  All as he turn'd him roun'—
" Farewell to Leader's silver tide !
  Farewell to Ercildoune !"

The hart and hind approach'd the place,
  As lingering yet he stood ;
And there, before Lord Douglas' face,
  With them he cross'd the flood.

Lord Douglas leap'd on his berry-brown steed,
  And spurred him the Leader o'er ;
But though he rode with lightning speed,
  He never saw them more.

Some said to hill, and some to glen,
  Their wond'rous course had been ;
But ne'er in haunts of living men
  Again was Thomas seen.

SIR WALTER SCOTT.

KILMENY.

BONNIE Kilmeny gaed up the glen ;
But it wasna to meet Duneira's men,
Nor the rosy monk of the isle to see,
For Kilmeny was pure as pure could be.
It was only to hear the yorling sing,
And pu' the cress-flower round the spring ;
The scarlet hypp and the hind-berrye,
And the nest that hung frae the hazel-tree ;
For Kilmeny was pure as pure could be.

But lang may her minny look o'er the wa' ;
And lang may she seek i' the greenwood shaw ;
Lang the Laird o' Duneira blame,
And lang, lang greet or Kilmeny come hame !

When many lang day had come and fled,
When grief grew calm and hope was dead,
When mass for Kilmeny's soul had been sung,
When the bedesman had prayed and the dead-bell
    rung,
Late, late in a gloaming, when all was still,
When the fringe was red on the westlin hill,
The wood was sere, the moon i' the wane,
The reek o' the cot hung o'er the plain,
Like a little wee cloud in the world its lane ;
When the ingle lowed wi' an eiry leme—
Late, late in the gloaming, Kilmeny came hame !

" Kilmeny, Kilmeny, where have you been ?
Lang hae we sought baith holt and dean ;
By burn, by ford, by greenwood tree,
Yet you are halesome and fair to see.
Where gat ye that joup o' the lily sheen ?
That bonnie snood o' the birk sae green ?
And those roses, the fairest that ever were seen ?
Kilmeny, Kilmeny, where have you been ? "

Kilmeny look'd up wi' a lovely grace,
But nae smile was seen on Kilmeny's face ;
As still was her look, and as still was her e'e,
As the stillness that lay on the emerant lea,
Or the mist that sleeps on a waveless sea.
For Kilmeny had been, she kenned not where,
And Kilmeny had seen what she could not declare ;
Kilmeny had been where the cock never crew,
Where the rain never fell, and the wind never blew.

But it seemed as the harp of the sky had rung,
And the airs of heaven played round her tongue,
When she spoke of the lovely forms she had seen,
And a land where sin had never been ;
A land of love and a land of light,
Withouten sun, or moon, or night,
Where the river swa'd a living stream,
And the light a pure and cloudless beam ;
The land of vision it would seem,
A still, an everlasting dream.

In yon greenwood there is a waik,
And in that waik there is a wene,
    And in that wene that is a maike ;
That neither has flesh, nor blood, nor bane ;
And down in yon greenwood he walks his lane.

In that green wene Kilmeny lay,
Her bosom hap'd wi' flowerets gay ;
But the air was soft, and the silence deep,
And bonny Kilmeny fell sound asleep.
She kenned na mair, nor open'd her e'e,
Till wak'd by the hymns of a far countrye.

She woke on a couch of silk sae slim,
All striped wi' the bars of the rainbow's rim ;
And lovely beings round were rife,
Who erst had travelled mortal life ;
And aye they smiled and 'gan to speer,
" What spirit hath brought this mortal here ? "

" Lang have I rang'd the world wide,"
A meek and reverend fere replied ;
" Baith night and day I have watched the fair,
Eident a thousand years and mair.

Yes, I have watched o'er ilk degree,
Wherever blooms feminitye ;
And sinless virgin, free of stain
In mind and body, found I nane.
Never since the banquet of time
Found I a virgin in her prime,
Till late this bonnie maiden I saw,
As spotless as the morning snaw ;
Full twenty years she has lived as free
As the spirits that sojourn in this countrye :
I have brought her away from the snares of men,
That sin or death she never may ken."

They clasped her waist, and her hands sae fair,
They kissed her cheeks and they kemmed her hair ;
And round came many a blooming fere,
Saying, " Bonnie Kilmeny, ye're welcome here !
Women are freed of the littand scorn,
O blessed be the day Kilmeny was born !
Now shall the land of the spirits see,
Now shall it ken what a woman may be !
Many lang year, in sorrow and pain,
Many lang year through the world we've gane,
Commissioned to watch fair woman-kind,
For it's they who nurse the immortal mind.
We have watched their steps as the dawning shone,
And deep in the greenwood walks alone ;
By lily bower and silken bed,
The viewless tears have been o'er them shed ;
Have soothed their ardent minds to sleep,
Or left the couch of love to weep.
We have seen, we have seen ! but the time maun come,
And the angels will weep at the day of doom !

" O would the fairest of mortal kind
Aye keep these holy truths in mind,

That kindred spirits their motions see,
Who watch their ways with anxious e'e,
And grieve for the guilt of humanitye !
O, sweet to Heaven the maiden's prayer,
And the sigh that heaves a bosom sae fair !
And dear to heaven the words of truth
And the praise of virtue from beauty's mouth !
And dear to the viewless forms of air,
The mind that kythes as the body fair.

"O, bonny Kilmeny ! free frae stain,
If ever you seek the world again,
That world of sin, of sorrow, and fear,
O tell of the joys that are waiting here ;
And tell of the signs you shall shortly see ;
Of the times that are now, and the times that shall be.

They lifted Kilmeny, they led her away,
And she walked in the light of a sunless day ;
The sky was a dome of crystal bright,
The fountain of vision and fountain of light ;
The emerant fields were of dazzling glow,
And the flowers of everlasting blow.
Then deep in the stream her body they laid,
That her youth and her beauty never might fade ;
And they smil'd on Heaven when they saw her lie
In the stream of life that wandered by.
And she heard a song, she heard it sung,
She ken'd not where, but sae sweetly it rung,
It fell on the ear like a dream of the morn, —
"O, blest be the day that Kilmeny was born !
Now shall the land of the spirits see,
Now shall it ken what a woman may be !
The sun that shines on the world sae bright,
A borrowed gleid frae the fountain of light ;

And the moon that sleeks the sky sae dun,
Like a gouden bow or a beamless sun,
Shall wear away and be seen nae mair,
And the angels shall miss them travelling the air.
But lang, lang after, baith nicht and day,
When the sun and the world have fled away ;
When the sinner has gone to his waesome doom,
Kilmeny shall smile in eternal bloom ! "

They bore her away, she wist not how,
For she felt not arm nor rest below ;
But so swift they wained her through the light,
'Twas like the motion of sound or sight ;
They seemed to split the gales of air,
And yet nor gale nor breeze was there.
Unnumbered groves below them grew,
They came, they passed, and backward flew,
Like floods of blossoms gliding on,
A moment seen, in a moment gone.
Ah ! never vales to mortal view
Appeared like those o'er which they flew,
That land to human spirits given,
The lowermost vales of the storied heaven ;
From thence they can view the world below,
And heaven's blue gates with sapphires glow,
More glory yet unmeet to know.

They bore her far to a mountain green,
To see what mortal never had seen,
And they seated her high on a purple sward,
And bade her heed what she saw and heard,
And note the changes the spirits wrought,
For now she lives in the land of thought.
She looked, and she saw nor sun nor skies,
But a crystal dome of a thousand dyes :
She looked, and she saw nae land aright,

But an endless whirl of glory and light,
And radiant beings went and came,
Far swifter than wind, or the linkèd flame.
She hid her e'en frae the dazzling view ;
She looked again, and the scene was new.
She saw a sun in a summer sky,
And clouds of amber sailing by ;
A lovely land beneath her lay,
And that land had lakes and mountains grey ;
And that land had valleys and hoary piles,
And marled seas and a thousand isles.
Its fields were speckled, its forests green,
And its lakes were all of the dazzling sheen,
Like magic mirrors, where shining lay,
The sun, and the sky, and the cloudlet grey ;
Which heaved and trembled and gently swung,
On every shore they seemed to be hung :
For there they were seen on their downward plain
A thousand times and a thousand again ;
In winding lake and placid firth,
Like peaceful heavens in the bosom of earth.

Kilmeny sighed and seemed to grieve,
For she found her heart to that land did cleave ;
She saw the corn wave in the vale ;
She saw the deer run down the dale ;
She saw the plaid and the broad claymore,
And the brows that the badge of freedom bore,—
And she thought she had seen the land before.

She saw a lady sit on a throne,
The fairest that ever the sun shone on :
A lion licked her hand of milk,
And she held him in a leish of silk ;
And a leifu' maiden stood at her knee,
With a silver wand and melting e'e ;

Her sovereign shield till love stole in,
And poisoned all the fount within.
Then a gruff, untoward bedesman came,
And hundit the lion on his dame;
And the guardian maid wi' the dauntless e'e,
She dropped a tear, and left her knee;
And she saw till the queen frae the lion fled,
Till the bonniest flower o' the world lay dead;
A coffin was set on a distant plain,
And she saw the red blood fall like rain;
Then bonny Kilmeny's heart grew sair,
And she turned away, and could look nae mair.

Then the gruff, grim carle girned amain,
And they trampled him down, but he rose again;
And he bated the lion to deeds of weir,
Till he lapped the blood to the kingdom dear;
And, weening his head was danger preef,
When crowned with the rose and clover leaf,
He gowled at the carle, and chased him away,
To feed wi' the deer on the mountain grey.
He gowled at the carl, and he gecked at heaven,
But his mark was set and his arles given,
Kilmeny a while her e'en withdrew;
She looked again, and the scene was new.

She saw before her fair unfurled
One-half of all the glowing world,
Where oceans rolled, and rivers ran,
To bound the aims of sinful man.
She saw a people, fierce and fell,
Burst frae their bonds like fiends of hell;
There lilies grew, and the eagle flew:
And she herkèd on her ravening crew,
Till the cities and towers were wrapped in a blaze,

And the thunder it roared o'er the lands and the seas.
The widows wailed, and the red blood ran,
And she threatened an end to the race of man ;
She never loved, nor stood in awe,
Till caught by the lion's deadly paw.
Oh ! then the eagle swinked for life,
And brainzelled up a mortal strife ;
But flew she north, or flew she south,
She met wi' the gowl o' the lion's mouth.

With a mooted wing and waefu' maen,
The eagle sought her eiry again :
But lang may she cower in her bloody nest,
And lang, lang sleek her wounded breast,
Before she sey another flight,
To play wi' the norland lion's might.

But to sing the sights Kilmeny saw,
So far surpassing nature's law,
The singer's voice wad sink away,
And the string of his harp wad cease to play.
But she saw till the sorrows of man were by,
And all was love and harmony ;—
Till the stars of heaven fell calmly away,
Like flakes of snaw on a winter day.

Then Kilmeny begged again to see
The friends she had left in her ain countrie,
To tell of the place where she had been,
And the glories that lay in the land unseen ;
To warn the living maidens fair,
The loved of heaven, the spirits' care,
That all whose minds unmeled remain
Shall bloom in beauty when time is gane.
With distant music, soft and deep,

They lulled Kilmeny sound asleep ;
And when she awakened, she lay her lane,
All happed with flowers, in the greenwood wene.
When seven long years had come and fled,
When grief was calm, and hope was dead,
When scarce was remembered Kilmeny's name,
Late, late in a gloamin' Kilmeny came hame.
And O, her beauty was fair to see,
But still and steadfast was her e'e !
Such beauty bard may never declare,
For there was no pride nor passion there ;
And the soft desire of maiden's e'en
In that mild face could never be seen.
Her seymar was the lily flower,
And her cheek the moss-rose in the shower ;
And her voice like the distant melodye
That floats along the twilight sea.
But she loved to raike the lanely glen,
And keep afar frae the haunts of men,
Her holy hymns unheard to sing,
To suck the flowers, and drink the spring ;
But wherever her peaceful form appeared
The wild beasts of the hill were cheered ;
The wolf played blithely round the field,
The lordly byson lowed and kneeled ;
The dun deer wooed with manner bland,
And cowered beneath her lily hand.
And when at eve the woodlands rung,
When hymns of other worlds she sung
In ecstacy of sweet devotion,
O, then the glen was all in motion !
The wild beasts of the forest came,
Broke from their boughs and faulds the tame,
And goved around, charmed and amazed ;
Even the dull cattle crooned and gazed,
And murmured, and looked with anxious pain

For something the mystery to explain.
The buzzard came with the throstle-cock ;
The corby left her houf in the rock ;
The blackbird alang wi' the eagle flew ;
The hind came tripping over the dew ;
The wolf and the kid their raike began,
And the kid and the lamb and the leveret ran ;
The hawk and the hern attour them hung,
And the merle and the mavis forhooyed their young;
And all in a peaceful ring were hurled—
It was like an eve in a sinless world !

When a month and a day had come and gane,
Kilmeny sought the greenwood wene ;
There laid her down on the leaves sae green,
And Kilmeny on earth was never mair seen.
But O, the words that fell frae her mouth
Were words of wonder, and words of truth !
But all the land were in fear and dread,
For they kendna whether she was living or dead.
It wasna her hame, and she couldna remain ;
She left this world of sorrow and pain,
And returned to the land of thought again.

JAMES HOGG.

A FAIRY TALE.

ONCE in days of yore a little Princess, who had summers
    seen
Scarcely seven, and was christened by the holy name
    Christine,
Found herself, at eve, disporting in a fairy ring of green.

She had left the kingly castle; left her sire's and mother's
    side,
Left the banquet, where her brother feasted with his royal
    bride;
And had rambled to the forest valley, 'neath the summer
    moon,
Where she crossed the charmèd circle, aught thereof
    unknowing. Soon
Overwearied there she rested, wishing what might come
    to pass,
When by chance her hand alighted on a tuft of clover-
    grass.
This she grasped, a tiny handful :—Ah! Saint Mary!
    what she saw !—
Mounted on their milk-white palfreys, issuing from the
    shady shawe,
Came the fairies, caracolling gaily as they passed
    along;
Then, dismounting, closed around her in a bright and
    joyous throng;
Ladylings and lordlings dancing, piping, harping, full of
    song.
Clad in robes of silken silver, golden gossamer a few,
Decked with jewels bright as starlets, bright as berries,
    bright as dew;
Some in kirtle, scarf, and doublet, all of verdant forest
    hue.

Lovers there she saw, arm-twining, in the wild wood's
    shadowy slade;
There some woful knight was kneeling at the feet of
    haughty maid;
Here was feasting, there was music; many a cunning
    prank was played.

Suddenly, the stateliest of them, he that most a monarch
    seemed,
(Cap of crimson his, and mantle like an emerald that
    beamed)
When he spied the gentle maiden, smiling on the merry
    scene ;
" Ho ! my lords and ladies !" cried he, "wist ye who with
    us hath been ?
Lo ! a mortal stands among us ; fairer than a fairy she ;
Let us speak with her a moment ; questioning belongs to
    me."

Straight the jocund throng desisted from their pastime
    and their play,
While the king of all the fairies to the childling thus 'gan
    say :—

" Lovely mortal ! wilt thou, wilt thou quit with us thy
    childhood's bowers,
And in our enchanted Eden wander through a world of
    flowers ?
All delights that thou hast dreamed of, gathered there
    shall be, and thine ;
Flowers that fade not, games that end not, skies that
    always mildliest shine ;
Kneaded cates of amber honey, and the rosebud's dewy
    wine ;
Wreaths of jewels, combs of silver, beads and bracelets
    all of gold,
And a diamond girdle round thee ; mine I give thee
    now, behold !
Bowls of rubies thou shalt sip from, and from crystal
    tables dine,
An 1, at eve, on lily leaves, and mingled violets recline ;
Wilt thou with me, sweet one, tell me !" "King," she
    answered, "I am thine."

All the fairy court with rapture danced when thus they
    heard her say ;
"Noble chieftain, child of beauty, let us haste," they
    cried, "away ! "

"Seal the covenant first," quoth Oberon ; and a magic
    cup of wine
Straight was brought him, when the king bethought him
    of the charm divine,
Which the eyes of life had opened, to perceive their
    secret line.
Deep within the rosy goblet he the four-fold leaflet
    dipped,
Drank thereof, and to the damsel gave it ; daintily she
    sipped.

Then to horse ; the gallant knighthood lift their ladies to
    the sells ;
Every steed was shod with silver, every bridle hung with
    bells,
Like the lilies of the valley, only all of silver. Swells
Soft the moonlight air with strains aforetime never
    heard ;
More sweet than tone of nymph, or muse, or god, to both
    preferred.

So they ambled on until they reached a green and grove-
    crowned hill,
Which, without a gate, they entered, opening at the
    monarch's will :
Then the portals closed upon her ; woe is me for that
    dear child,
'Mid the insubstantial regions of the fairies thus beguiled.

Streams of bubbling gold flowed round her; fountains
flung their diamond spray,
O'er the fields a pearl-dew glistened ; polished loadstone
paved the way;
Trees were leafed with golden florins; daisies chimed
like silver crowns,
Musical and odorous breezes breathed across the velvet
downs.
Soon they neared the regal palace twinkling in the aëry
dyes,
Lilac, pearl, and beryl blended, of that country's sunless
skies ;
While the fay-queen and her ladies, with their flower-
robed damsels fair,
Came forthright to greet her crowned spouse, and royal
guestling there.

From the centre of the high dome swung a topaz solar
bright,
Which through all the palace darted gleams of glad and
glorious light,
Emerald lamplets ranked around it, tempered this with
cooler ray ;
While, without, the welkin poured one pale and ever-
dawning day.
There the feast was flowing ever; stream-like music
ceaseless played ;
There the dance was always weaving ; minstrels chanting
in the shade ;
There for aye the chase was bounding over dale and hill
and plain,
And fair Christine, on hound-high steed, the foremost of
the elfin train.
Still she saddened when she minded of the simple
garlands she

Wove of wild rose and of woodbine, with her playmates
    on the lea ;
And the hazel and brown beech nut which they gathered
    from the tree.
What though clad in jewelled raiment, trilling, tripping,
    day and night,
What though ply'd with queenly dainties, what though
    culling gold-blooms bright,
Never in the feast delicious, nor the dance's 'wildering
    whirl,
Nor the wine-cups merry orbit, could forget that lonely
    girl
The ancient hall where dwelled her sire, and, where,
    too, from her mother's side,
She, one summer's eve, had stolen forth into the forest
    wide.

" Drink the dew," the Fairy Fate said, "that the poppy
    lends repose,
Mingled with the fragrant nectar chaliced in the golden
    rose."
Then she drank the draught Lethean from the bowl with
    flowerets crowned,
Flaming flowers, that all remembrance of her past
    existence drowned ;
Thus, with lustres vainly lapsing, to perpetual childhood
    bound.
Never moon there marked the season ; sun ne'er
    shadowed forth the time ;
Years themselves were undistinguished in that soft and
    listless clime.

Now where mines of gold and silver branch, in many a
    gleaming vein,
Through the bosom of the mountain, 'neath the many
    leaguéd plain ;

Where jasper and cornelian clear and alabaster pure,
And purple spars and glass-bright rocks the glittering
    caves immure,
She roamed ; and all the virtues learned of every potent
    gem
Or mystic or medicinal ; all gifts that unto them
Pertained of causing love, or hate, or infinite delight,
Imperial wealth, tyrannic state, long life, and beauty
    bright ;
These into an armlet stringing, ruby, sapphire, emerald,
    pearl,
Threaded on the sunny tendril of one desultory curl,
As an amulet Titania gave to her, the spell-bound girl.

Through the dwarf-king's wondrous regions she with him
    delighted strayed ;
Rings and charms and magic weapons he for her, love-
    smitten, made.
Blythely oft beneath the seas she roved with mermaids
    from their caves,
Arched, with amber, pearl and ivory roofs, whose floor
    bright coral paves ;
And oft, too, when the fairy court, for pleasure, or for
    pride,
Would seek the cooling streams that lave earth's plains
    and meadows wide,
The water spirits, in their arms, the darling maid would
    fold,
And hidden things of years to come mysteriously they told :
There she viewed in crystal vases souls of hapless
    wretches drowned,
Which from their pellucid prisons she with holy zeal
    unbound ;
Upward sprang the sprites with joyful some, and some
    with mournful sound.

With the sylphs in air she sported; with the golden-
    palaced gnome,
Earth embosomed, or the light elves in their rainbow-
    clouded home.
Ofttimes with the Elle-King rode she, in his chariot,
    o'er the main,
While his martial band, with sea-conchs, blew the war-
    inspiring strain;
Then upon the headlands landing, counted o'er the frosty
    meads,
Royal droves of great blue kine, lipping the ice-dew of
    weeds.

'Gainst the fairies of the fire she with tidal spirits waged
War; and earth, and air, and ocean felt how fierce the
    battle raged.
High she shook her shining falchion, pliant as the rushen
    plant,
Falchion her dwarf-lover forged her, hard and bright as
    adamant;
Fighting by the Elle-King's side, there she the lord of
    fireland slew;
All the hosts of fire were routed; crowned her queen the
    conquering crew;
Back to fairyland she hasted; home her train in triumph
    drew.

King and spouse majestic welcome gave her, on her glad
    return;
And a thousand tongues besought that her adventures
    they might learn.
This she grants; and lo! a banquet, by unheard
    command is seen,
Instantaneously furnished on the flower-embroidered
    green.

On the east hand of her liege lord sat the bright, the
    brave Christine ;
On the west divine Titania, night's incomparable queen ;
Then the Victress told Sir Oberon all she had done, and
    where had been ;

How from end to end of faerie she had passed, below,
    above,
Scathless by the spells the dwarf-king gave her in his
    days of love ;
How had dealt with Nisses, Noks, and Kobolds,
    Kelpies, Norns, and Trolls ;
How with Peris fared, and Shadim, Afrits, Ogres, Deevs
    and Ghouls ;
She had travelled in the whirlwind ; for no harm to her
    might fall,
Who had talismans and virtues could enchant or vanquish
    all ;—
How the Elle-chief's broad dominions scarred by war,
    she sad, beheld ;
How with hosts of fire they fought, and how the first of
    foes she quelled ;
How, she said, in God she trusted ;—at that word the
    banquet ceased ;
Shrieked and vanished all the faërie, save the king who
    bade the feast.

Silent sate the maid and monarch many a moment, till,
    quoth he,
"Knowest thou not, unhappy child, the woe thou hast
    wrought in faërie?
Know'st thou not that by the name which elfin tongue
    hath never passed,
When so uttered, we are scattered, dust-like by the
    tempest's blast ;

Know'st thou not that we be spirits, doomed to linger
  here, unchanged,
In the sunless land of Faërie, from the light of heaven
  estranged,
Till with promise of salvation, we be blessed by holy priest,
Or some sinless mortal give us hope to be at last released?
Till the universal judgment we, the viewless sons of Eve,
Wander in the hollow underworld, unable to believe,
Till we hold the great assurance, for the lack whereof we
  grieve.

Still as we of sin were guiltless, save the sin inherited
From our mother's first transgression, ere the floods
  abroad were spread,
He, the great Creator, hid us in the bosom-shades of earth,
And forbade that in the sunlight ever we should journey
  forth."
"Bounteous is He," said the maiden, "of illimitable
  grace ;
Nor would He have hid ye here, if good He meant not
  to your race."
"Ah, alas ! then, why delayeth He his merciful com-
  mand ? "
Sighed the fairy; "sooner blossom shall the sceptre in
  my hand ; "
Saying,—in the mold he wildly struck his white and
  star-tipped wand.

Scarce had he the sad word uttered when the peeled and
  polished rod
Bourgeoned forth in buds and blossoms, rooted in the
  mossy sod ;
"Lo ! a miracle," said Christine ; "trust ye henceforth,
  too, in God.
Rest ye sure His mercy broodeth over all the souls He
  made."

"We are spirits," groaned the fairy, "greatly of our end afraid;
Though a flickering hope inspires us with belief that we shall be
Joined, at last, with Him and Heaven, in His boundless clemencie."
"Be it," said she; "knew not I, nathless, so saintly your desire;
And if mine your royal sanction to reseek my loving sire,
IIe within his walls sustains, for mercy's sake, a godly frere,
Who to pious aspirations ever lends a pitying ear;
And will grant His sacred blessing to your nation; doubt it ne'er;
He will bless whate'er loves me; for I to him was alway dear."

"Speed thee earthwards," said the sovran, "speed thee, dearest child of light;"
On the instant, hosts of fairies warbling, darted into sight.
Airs delicious, such as mortal never heard from human hands,
Whispered loud from golden clarions, harped on strings of silver strands,
Strains triumphant, thrilled and echoed through those dim enchanted lands.
"Speed thee, heart of love," they faltered, "speed thee on thy star-taught way;
Bring to Oberon and his people hope of heaven and peace for aye."
"Ah! farewell, ye good and loyal," said the princess, stepping forth,
"Ne'er shall I forget your bounties, never see surpassed your worth;
If not pure enough for heaven, ye are far too pure for earth."

Towards the limits far of Faërie quick their anxious
    course they took,
And the hill she entered first self-opened like a magic
    book ;
Forth she peeped, and backward turning to bestow one
    farewell look,
Nothing saw she, nothing heard she, save a low and
    eërie wail
With the rustle of the greenwood blending and the sunset
    gale.

All was changed ; and she, deep sighing, tottered on her
    lonesome way,
Till she neared a stunted hamlet ; children at their
    twilight play,
As she stooped to raise a withering rosebud, by the path
    that lay,
Shyly tittering ; thus she spake them ; "Laugh ye at my
    fresh-pulled roses ?"
"We laughed to see an old, old beldame picking up our
    cast off posies,"
Said they ; but she understood no word of what the
    bantlings uttered ;
And again they mouthed and mocked at that they said
    the old crone muttered.

Soon she came where, blind with dotage, propped on
    staff, an old man stood ;
All his tresses white with age as with its snows a wintry
    wood.
"Gaffer," said she, " where's the castle, that on yonder
    mountain piled
Held the prince unpeered in honour ? Late I left it,
    foolish child !"
Mused a moment, recollecting ; presently, the old man
    smiled :

"Second childhood then I fancy must at least, good
    dame, be thine;
I alone in all the region mind me of that lordly line;
I alone some words remember of the tongue that then
    was spoke,
By the noble race that here dwelt, ere they felt war's
    iron yoke.
King, peer, peasant, all were conquered, all uprooted at
    a blow;
One disastrous battle gave the country to a foreign foe;
Slain or banished all; but that's well-nigh a hundred
    years ago.

"Yonder castle's crumbling ruin saw its lord, though
    dauntless, fall;
Dame and daughter he beheld both slain; in vain his
    vassals all,
In vain his son for crown and bride fought; he was left
    an idiot thrall.
On the evening of his bridal, souls of war, those sea-
    kings came,
And, ere midnight, tower and town were all engulphed
    in gory flame.
Save the holy chaplain, none of all that princely house
    remained,
And myself, the humblest menial, on the lands where
    once they reigned.
He, in rock-hewn hermit's cavern, life, with passion
    undefiled,
Wore away, in trances murmuring blessings on some
    wandered child,
Daughter of his Lord, 'twas counted, by the cursed
    invading host
Killed; or wiled away by fairies; howsoe'er, the child
    was lost.

Twenty winters since his clay from mine to earth's cold
arms was given ; [heaven."
And so long his blessed spirit has been with the saints in

"Hold," she cried, "I hear a weeping; I no longer
love the light ; "
Back she started, and departed straightways through the
deepening night.
In the hill she heard a wailing and a sobbing sad and deep;
And the crash of thousand harpstrings hands of desper-
ation sweep ;
Then she laid her down, and, praying, slept the long
unmorrowing sleep.

PHILIP JAMES BAILEY.

THE CONQUEST OF FAIRYLAND.

THERE reigned a king in the land of Persia, mighty and
great was he grown,
On the necks of the kings of the conquered earth he
builded up his throne.

There sate a king on the throne of Persia ; and he was
grown so proud
That all the life of the world was less, to him, than a
passing cloud.

He reigned in glory : joy and sorrow lying between his
hands.
If he sighed a nation shook, his smile ripened the harvest
of lands.

He was the saddest man beneath the everlasting sky,
For all his glories had left him old, and the proudest
king must die.

He who was even as God to all the nations of men,
Must die as the merest peasant dies, and turn into earth
    again.

And his life with the fear of death was bitter and sick
    and accursed,
As brackish water to drink of which is to be for ever
    athirst.

The hateful years rolled on and on, but once it chanced
    at noon
The drowsy court was thrilled to gladness, it echoed so
    sweet a tune.

Low as the lapping of the sea, as the song of the lark is
    clear,
Wild as the moaning of pine branches ; the king was
    fain to hear.

" What is the song, and who is the singer? " he said ;
    " before the throne
Let him come, for the songs of the world are mine, and
    all but this are known."

Seven mighty kings went out the Minstrel man to find :
And all they found was a dead cypress soughing in the
    wind.

And slower still, and sadder still the heavy winters
    rolled,
And the burning summers waned away, and the king
    grew very old ;

Dull, worn, feeble, bent ; and once he thought, " To die
Were rest, at least." And, as he thought, the music
    wandered by.

Into the presence of the king, singing, the singer came,
And his face was like the spring in flower, his eyes were
clear as flame.

"What is the song you play, and what the theme your
praises sing?
It is sweet ; I knew not I owned a thing so sweet," said
the weary king.

"I sing my country," said the singer, "a land that is
sweeter than song."
"Which of my kingdoms is your country? Thither
would I along."

"Great, O king, is thy power, and the earth a footstool
for thy feet ;
But my country is free, and my own country, and oh, my
country is sweet !"

The eyes of the king, as he heard, grew young and alive
with fire :
"So, is there left on the earth a thing to strive for, a
thing to desire?

"Where is thy country? tell me, O singer ! speak thine
innermost heart !
Leave thy music ! speak plainly ! Speak – forget thine
art !"

The eyes of the singer shone as he sang, and his voice
rang wild and free
As the elemental wind or the uncontrollable sobs of the
sea.

"O for my distant home !" he sighed ; "Oh, alas !
away and afar
I watch thee now as a lost sailor watches a shining star.

"Oh that a wind would take me there! that a bird
  would set me down
Where the golden streets shine red at sunset in my
  father's town!

"For only in dreams I see the faces of the women there,
And fain would I hear them singing once, braiding their
  ropes of hair.

"Oh I am thirsty and long to drink of the river of life,
  and I
Am fain to find my own country, where no man shall
  die."

Out of the light of the throne, the king looked down : as
  in the spring
The green leaves burst from their dusky buds, so was
  hope in the eyes of the king.

"Lo," he said, "I will make thee great; I will make
  thee mighty in sway
Even as I ; but the name of thy country speak, and the
  place and the way."

"Oh, the way to my country is ever north till you pass
  the mouth of hell,
Past the limbo of dreams and the desolate land where
  shadows dwell.

"And when you have reached the fount of wonder, you
  ford the waters wan
To the land of elves and the land of fairies, enchanted
  Masinderan."

The singer ceased ; and the lyre in his hand snapped, as
a cord, in twain ;
And neither lyre nor singer was seen in the kingdom of
Persia again.

And all the nobles gazed astounded ; no man spoke a
word
Till the old King said : "Call out my armies ; bring me
hither a sword ! "

As a little torrent swollen by snows is turned to a terrible
stream,
So the gathering voices of all his countries cried to the
king in his dream.

Crying, "For thee, O our king, for thee, we had freely
and willingly died,
Warriors, martyrs, what thou wilt ; not that our lives
betide

"The worth of a thought to the king, but rather, O
ruler, because thy rod
Is over our heads, as over thine is the changeless will of
God.

"Rather for this we beseech thee, O master, for thine
own sake refrain
From the blasphemous madness of pride, from the fever
of impious gain."

"You seek my death" the king thundered ; "you cry,
Forbear to save
The life of a king too old to frolic ; let him drowse in the
grave.

" But I will live for all your treason ; and, by my own
   right hand !
I will set out this day with you to conquer Fairyland ! "

Then all the nations paled aghast, for the battle to begin
Was a war with God, and a war with death, and they
   knew the thing was sin.

Sick at heart they gathered together, but none denounced
   the wrong,
For the will of God was unseen, unsaid, and the will of
   the king was strong.

So the air grew bright with spears, and the earth shook
   under the tread
Of the mighty horses harnessed for battle ; the standards
   flaunted red.

And the wind was loud with the blare of trumpets, and
   every house was void
Of the strength and stay of the house, and the peace of
   the land destroyed.

And the growing corn was trodden under the weight of
   armèd feet,
And every woman in Persia cursed the sound of a song
   too sweet,

Cursed the insensate longing for life in the heart of a sick
   old man ;
But the King of Persia with all his armies marched on
   Masinderan.

Many a day they marched in the sun till their silver
   armour was lead
To sink their bodies into the grave, and many a man fell
   dead.

And they passed the mouth of hell, and the shadowy
country gray,
Where the air is mist and the people mist and the rain
more real than they.

And they came to the fount of wonder, and forded the
waters wan,
And the King of Persia and all his armies marched on
Masinderan.

And they turned the rivers to blood, and the fields to a
ravaged camp,
Till they neared the golden faery town, that burned in
the dusk as a lamp.

And they shouted and shouted for joy, to see it stand so
nigh,
Given into their hands for spoil ; and their hearts beat
proud and high.

The armies longed for the morrow, to conquer the
shining town,
For there was no death in the land, neither any to strike
them down.

And the hosts were many in numbers, mighty, and
skilled in the strife,
And they lusted for gold and conquest as the old king
lusted for life.

Till, gazing on the golden place, night took them
unaware,
And black and windy grew the skies, and black the
eddying air—

So long the night and black the night that fell upon their
    eyes,
They quaked with fear, those mighty hosts; the sun
    would never rise.

Darkness and deafening sounds confused the black,
    tempestuous air,
And no man saw his neighbour's face, nor heard his
    neighbour's prayer.

And wild with terror the mad battalions fell on each
    other in fight,
The ground was strewn with wounded men, mad in the
    horrible night—

Mad with eternal pain, with darkness and stabbing
    blows
Rained on all sides from invisible hands till the ground
    was red as a rose.

And, though he were longing for rest, none ventured to
    pause from the strife,
Lest haply another wound be his to poison his hateful
    life.

And the king entreated death ; and for peace the armies
    prayed ;
But the gifts of God are everlasting, His word is not
    gainsayed.

Gold and battle are given the hosts, their boon is turned
    to a ban,
And the curse of the king is to live forever in conquered
    Masinderan.

                              A. MARY F. ROBINSON.

Men and Fairies.

THE APPROACH OF TITANIA.

PUCK.

Now the hungry lion roars,
　And the wolf behowls the moon !
Whilst the heavy ploughman snores,
　All with weary task fordone.
Now the wasted brands do glow,
　Whilst the scritch-owl, scritching loud,
Puts the wretch, that lies in woe,
　In remembrance of a shroud.
Now it is the time of night
　That the graves, all gaping wide,
Every one lets forth his sprite,
　In the churchyard paths to glide :
And we fairies, that do run
　By the triple Hecate's team,
From the presence of the sun,
　Following darkness like a dream,
Now are frolic : not a mouse
　Shall disturb this hallowed house :
I am sent with broom before,
　To sweep the dust behind the door.

Enter OBERON *and* TITANIA, *with their* Train.

OBERON.

Through this house give glimmering light,
　By the dead and drowsy fire :
Every elf and fairy sprite
　Hop as light as bird from briar ;
And this ditty, after me,
Sing, and dance it trippingly.

TITANIA.

First rehearse this song by rote :
To each word a warbling note,
Hand in hand, with fairy grace,
Will we sing, and bless this place.

Song and Dance.

OBERON.

Now, until the break of day,
Through this house each fairy stray ;
To the best bride-bed will we,
Which by us shall blessed be ;
And the issue there create
Ever shall be fortunate ;
So shall all the couples three
Ever true in loving be :
And the blots of nature's hand
Shall not in their issue stand ;
Never mole, hare-lip, nor scar,
Nor mark prodigious, such as are
Despised in nativity,
Shall upon their children be.—
With this field-dew consecrate,
Every fairy take his gait ;
And each several chamber bless,
Through this palace with sweet peace:
E'er shall it in safety rest,
And the owner of it blest.
   Trip away ;
   Make no stay :
Meet me all by break of day.

WILLIAM SHAKESPEARE.

A FAIRY TALE

IN THE ANCIENT ENGLISH STYLE.

IN Britain's Isle, in Arthur's days,
When midnight fairies daunc'd the maze,
    Liv'd Edwin of the Green ;
Edwin, I wis, a gentle youth,
Endow'd with courage, sense, and truth,
    Though badly shap'd he'd been.

His mountain back mote well be said,
To measure height against his head,
    And lift itself above ;
Yet, spite of all that Nature did
To make his uncouth form forbid,
    This creature dar'd to love.

He felt the charms of Edith's eyes,
Nor wanted hope to gain the prize,
    Could ladies look within ;
But one Sir Topaz dress'd with art,
And, if a shape could win a heart,
    He had a shape to win.

Edwin, if right I read my song,
With slighted passion pac'd along
    All in the moony light ;
'Twas near an old enchanted court,
Where sportive fairies made resort
    To revel out the night.

His heart was drear, his hope was cross'd,
'Twas late, 'twas far, the path was lost
    That reach'd the neighbour town ;

445

With weary steps he quits the shades,
Resolv'd, the darkling dome he treads,
    And drops his limbs adown.

But scant he lays him on the floor
When hollow winds remove the door,
    And trembling rocks the ground :
And, well I ween to count aright,
At once a hundred tapers light
    On all the walls around.

Now sounding tongues assail his ear,
Now sounding feet approachen near,
    And now the sounds increase :
And from the corner where he lay
He sees a train profusely gay
    Come prankling o'er the place.

But (trust me, Gentles !) never yet
Was dight a masquing half so neat,
    Or half so rich before ;
The country lent the sweet perfumes,
The sea the pearl, the sky the plumes,
    The town its silken store.

Now, whilst he gaz'd, a gallant drest
In flaunting robes above the rest,
    With awful accent cry'd ;
" What mortal of a wretched mind,
Whose sighs infect the balmy wind,
    Has here presum'd to hide ? "

At this the swain, whose venturous soul
No fears of magic art controul,
    Advanc'd in open sight ;

" Nor have I cause of dread," he said,
" Who view, by no presumption led,
   Your revels of the night.

" 'Twas grief, for scorn of faithful love,
Which made my steps ünweeting rove
   Amid the nightly dew."
" 'Tis well," the gallant cries again,
" We fairies never injure men
   Who dare to tell us true.

" Exalt thy love-dejected heart,
Be mine the task, or ere we part,
   To make thee grief resign ;
Now take the pleasure of thy chaunce ;
Whilst I with Mab, my partner, daunce,
   Be little Mable thine."

He spoke, and all a sudden there
Light music floats in wanton air ;
   The monarch leads the queen :
The rest their fairy partners found ;
And Mable trimly tript the ground
   With Edwin of the Green.

The daucing past, the board was laid,
And siker such a feast was made,
   As heart and lip desire,
Withouten hands the dishes fly,
The glasses with a wish come nigh,
   And with a wish retire.

But, now to please the fairy king,
Full every deal they daunce and sing,
   And antic feats devise ;

Some wind and tumble like an ape,
And other some transmute their shape
   In Edwin's wondering eyes.

Till one at last, that Robin hight,
Renown'd for pinching maids by night,
   Has bent him up aloof;
And full against the beam he flung,
Where by the back the youth he hung
   To sprawl uneath the roof.

From thence, " Reverse my charm," he cries,
" And let it fairly now suffice
   The gambol has been shewn."
But Oberon answers with a smile,
" Content thee, Edwin, for awhile,
   The vantage is thine own."

Here ended all the phantom-play ;
They smelt the fresh approach of day,
   And heard a cock to crow ;
The whirling wind that bore the crowd
Has clapp'd the door, and whistled loud,
   To warn them all to go.

Then screaming all at once they fly,
And all at once the tapers die ;
   Poor Edwin falls to floor ;
Forlorn his state, and dark the place,
Was never wight in such a case
   Through all the land before.

But soon as Dan Apollo rose,
Full jolly creature home he goes,
   He feels his back the less ;

His honest tongue and steady mind
Had rid him of the lump behind,
   Which made him want success.

With lusty livelyhed he talks,
He seems advancing as he walks,
   His story soon took wind ;
And beauteous Edith sees the youth
Endowed with courage, sense, and truth,
   Without a bunch behind.

The story told, Sir Topaz mov'd,
The youth of Edith erst approv'd,
   To see the revel scene :
At close of eve he leaves his home,
And wends to find the ruin'd dome
   All on the gloomy plain.

And there he bides, it so befel,
The wind came rustling down a dell,
   A shaking seized the wall ;
Up spring the tapers as before,
The fairies bragly foot the floor,
   And music fills the hall.

But certes sorely sunk with woe
Sir Topaz sees the Elphin show,
   His spirits in him die ;
When Oberon crys, " A man is near,
A mortal passion, cleeped fear,
   Hangs flagging in the sky."

With that, Sir Topaz, hapless youth !
In accents faultering, aye for ruth,
   Intreats them pity grant ;

For als he been a mister wight
Betray'd by wandering in the night
    To tread the circled haunt ;

"A Losell vile," at once they roar,
" And little skill'd of fairy lore,
    Thy cause to come we know ;
Now has thy kestrel courage fell,
And fairies, since a lie you tell,
    Are free to work thee woe."

Then Will, who bears the wispy fire
To trail the swains among the mire,
    The caitiff upward flung ;
There, like a tortoise in a shop,
He dangled from the chamber top,
    Where whilome Edwin hung.

The revel now proceeds apace,
Deftly they strut it o'er the place,
    They sit, they drink, and eat ;
The time with frolic mirth beguile,
And poor Sir Topaz hangs the while
    Till all the rout retreat.

By this the stars began to wink,
They shriek, they fly, the tapers sink,
    And down y-drops the knight :
For never spell by fairy laid
With strong enchantment bound a glade,
    Beyond the length of night.

Chill, dark, alone, adreed, he lay,
Till up the welkin rose the day,
    Then deem'd the dole was o'er :

But wot ye well his harder lot?
His seely back the bunch had got
   Which Edwin lost afore.

This tale a Sybil-nurse ared ;
She softly stroak'd my youngling head,
   And when the tale was done,
" Thus some are born, my son," she cries,
" With base impediments to rise,
   And some are born with none.

" But virtue can itself advance
To what the favourite fools of chance
   By fortune seem'd design'd ;
Virtue can gain the odds of fate,
And from itself shake off the weight
   Upon th' unworthy mind."

               THOMAS PARNELL.

THE ELFIN KING.

" O SWIFT and swifter far he speeds
   Than earthly steed can run ;
But I hear not the feet of his courser fleet,
   As he glides o'er the moorland dun."

Lone was the strath where he crossed their path,
   And wide did the heath extend,
The Knight in Green on that moor is seen
   At every seven years' end.

And swift is the speed of his coal-black steed,
　As the leaf before the gale,
But never yet have that courser's feet
　Been heard on hill or dale.

But woe to the wight who meets the Green Knight,
　Except on his faulchion arm
Spell-proof he bear, like the brave St. Clair,
　The holy Trefoil's charm ;

For then shall fly his gifted eye,
　Delusions false and dim ;
And each unblessed shade shall stand portrayed
　In ghostly form and limb.

O swifter, and swifter far he speeds
　Than earthly steed can run ;
"He skims the blue air," said the brave St. Clair,
　"Instead of the heath so dun.

"His locks are as bright as the streamer's light,
　His cheeks like the rose's hue ;
The Elfin-King, like the merlin's wing
　Are his pinions of glossy blue."

"No Elfin-King, with azure wing,
　On the dark brown moor I see ;
But a courser keen, and a Knight in Green,
　And full fair I ween is he.

"Nor Elfin-King, nor azure wing,
　Nor ringlets sparkling bright ;"
Sir Geoffrey cried, and forward hied
　To join the stranger Knight.

He knew not the path of the lonely strath,
    Where the Elfin-King went his round ;
Or he never had gone with the Green Knight on,
    Nor trod the charmèd ground.

How swift they flew ! no eye could view
    Their track on heath or hill ;
Yet swift across both moor and moss
    St. Clair did follow still.

And soon was seen a circle green,
    Where a shadowy wassel crew
Amid the ring did dance and sing,
    In weeds of watchet blue.

And the windlestrae,* so limber and grey,
    Did shiver beneath the tread
Of the coursers' feet, as they rushed to meet
    The morrice of the dead.

"Come here, come here, with thy green fere,
    Before the bread be stale ;
To roundel dance with speed advance,
    And taste our wassel ale."

Then up to the Knight came a grizly wight,
    And sounded in his ear,
"Sir Knight, eschew this goblin crew,
    Nor taste their ghostly cheer."

The tabors rung, the lilts were sung,
    And the Knight the dance did lead ;
But the maidens fair seemed round him to stare,
    With eyes like the glassy bead.

              * Rye-grass.

The glance of their eye, so cold and so dry,
    Did almost his heart appal ;
Their motion is swift, but their limbs they lift
    Like stony statues all.

Again to the Knight came the grizly wight,
    When the rounded dance was o'er ;
" Sir Knight, eschew this goblin crew,
    Or rue for evermore."

But forward pressed the dauntless guest
    To the tables of ezlar red,
And there was seen the Knight in Green,
    To grace the fair board head.

And before that Knight was a goblet bright
    Of emerald smooth and green,
The fretted brim was studded full trim
    With mountain rubies' sheen.

Sir Geoffrey the Bold of the cup laid hold
    With health-ale mantling o'er ;
And he saw as he drank that the ale never shrank
    But mantled as before.

Then Sir Geoffrey grew pale as he quaffed the ale,
    And cold as the corpse of clay ;
And with horny beak the ravens did shriek,
    And fluttered o'er their prey.

But soon throughout the revel rout
    A strange commotion ran,
For beyond the round they heard the sound
    Of the steps of an uncharmed man.

And soon to St. Clair the grim wight did repair,
From the midst of the wassel crew ;
"Sir Knight, beware of the revellers there,
Nor do as they bid thee do."

"What woeful wight art thou ?" said the Knight,
"To haunt this wassel fray ?"
"I was once," quoth he, "a mortal, like thee,
Though now I'm an elfin grey.

"And the Knight so bold as the corpse lies cold,
Who trode the greensward ring ;
He must wander along with that restless throng,
For aye, with the Elfin-King.

"With the restless crew, in weeds so blue,
The hapless Knight must wend ;
Nor ever be seen on haunted green
Till the weary seven years' end.

"Fair is the mien of the Knight in Green,
And bright his sparkling hair ;
'Tis hard to believe how malice can live
In the breast of aught so fair.

"And light and fair are the fields of air,
Where he wanders to and fro ;
Still doomed to fleet from the regions of heat
To the realms of endless snow.

"When high overhead fall the streamers* red,
He views the blessed afar ;
And in stern despair darts through the air
To earth, like a falling star.

* Northern Lights.

" With his shadowy crew, in weeds so blue,
    That Knight for aye must run ;
Except thou succeed in a perilous deed,
    Unseen by the holy sun.

" Who ventures the deed, and fails to succeed,
    Perforce must join the crew."
" Then brief, declare," said the brave St. Clair,
    " A deed that a Knight may do."

" 'Mid the sleet and the rain thou must here remain
    By the haunted greensward ring,
Till the dance wax slow, and the song faint and low,
    Which the crew unearthly sing.

" Then right at the time of the matin chime,
    Thou must tread the unhallowed ground,
And with mystic pace the circles trace
    That inclose it nine times round.

" And next thou must pass the rank green grass
    To the tables of ezlar red ;
And the goblet clear away thou must bear,
    Nor behind thee turn thy head.

" And ever anon as thou treadest upon
    The sward of the green charmed ring,
Be no word expressed in that space unblessed
    That 'longeth of holy thing.

" For the charmed ground is all unsound,
    And the lake spreads wide below,
And the Water-Fiend there, with the Fiend of Air,
    Is leagued for mortals' woe."

'Mid the sleet and the rain did St. Clair remain
  Till the evening star did rise ;
And the rout so gay did dwindle away
  To the eldritch dwarfy size.

When the moonbeams pale fell through the white
    hail,
  With a wan and a watery ray,
Sad notes of woe seemed round him to grow,
  The dirge of the elfins grey.

And right at the time of the matin chime
  His mystic pace began,
And murmurs deep around him did creep
  Like the moans of a murdered man.

The matin bell was tolling farewell
  When he reached the central ring,
And there he beheld, to ice congealed,
  That crew, with the Elfin-King.

For aye, at the knell of the matin bell,
  When the black monks wend to pray,
The spirits unblessed have a glimpse of rest
  Before the dawn of day.

The sigh of the trees, and the rush of the breeze,
  Then pause on the lonely hill ;
And the frost of the dead clings round their head,
  And they slumber cold and still.

The Knight took up the emerald cup,
  And the ravens hoarse did scream,
And the shuddering elfins half rose up,
  And murmured in their dream :

They inwardly mourned, and the thin blood returned
　　To every icy limb;
And each frozen eye, so cold and so dry,
　　'Gan roll with lustre dim.

Then brave St. Clair did turn him there
　　To retrace the mystic track,
He heard the sigh of his lady fair,
　　Who sobbed behind his back.

He started quick and his heart beat thick,
　　And he listened in wild amaze;
But the parting bell on his ear it fell,
　　And he did not turn to gaze.

With panting breast as he forward pressed,
　　He trod on a mangled head;
And the skull did scream, and the voice did seem
　　The voice of his mother dead.

He shuddering trode: on the great name of God
　　He thought—but he nought did say;
And the greensward did shrink, as about to sink,
　　And loud laughed the Elfins grey.

And loud did resound, o'er the unblessed ground,
　　The wings of the blue Elf-King;
And the ghostly crew to reach him flew,
　　But he crossed the charméd ring;

The morning was grey, and dying away
　　Was the sound of the matin bell;
And far to the west the fays that ne'er rest,
　　Fled where the moonbeams fell.

And Sir Geoffrey the Bold, on the unhallowed
    mould,
  Arose from the green witch-grass ;
And he felt his limbs, like a dead man's, cold,
  And he wist not where he was.

And that cup so rare, which the brave St. Clair
  Did bear from the ghostly crew,
Was suddenly changed, from the emerald fair,
  To the ragged whinstone blue ;
And instead of the ale that mantled there
  Was the murky midnight dew.

JOHN LEYDEN.

THE YOUNG TAMLANE.

"O I FORBID ye, maidens a'
  That wear gowd on your hair,
To come or gae by Carterhaugh,
  For young Tamlane is there.

"There's nane that gaes by Carterhaugh,
  But maun leave him a wad,
Either gowd rings or green mantles,
  Or else their maidenheid.

"Now gowd rings ye may buy, maidens,
  Green mantles ye may spin ;
But, gin ye lose your maidenheid,
  Ye'll ne'er get that agen."—

But up then spake her, fair Janet,
   The fairest o' a' her kin ;
" I'll cum and gang to Carterhaugh,
   And ask nae leave o' him."

Janet has kilted her green kirtle,
   A little abune her knee ;
And she has braided her yellow hair,
   A little abune her bree.

And when she came to Carterhaugh,
   She gaed beside the well ;
And there she fand his steed standing,
   But away was himsell.

She hadna pu'd a red red rose,
   A rose but barely three ;
Till up and starts a wee wee man,
   At lady Janet's knee.

Says—" Why pu' ye the rose, Janet ?
   What gars ye break the tree ?
Or why come ye to Carterhaugh,
   Withouten leave o' me ? "—

Says—" Carterhaugh it is mine ain ;
   My daddie gave it me ;
I'll come and gang to Carterhaugh,
   And ask nae leave o' thee."

He's ta'en her by the milk-white hand,
   Among the leaves sae green ;
And what they did, I cannot tell—
   The green leaves were between.

He's ta'en her by the milk-white hand,
  Among the roses red ;
And what they did, I cannot say—
  She ne'er return'd a maid.

When she came to her father's ha',
  She looked pale and wan ;
They thought she'd dreed some sair sickness,
  Or been with some leman.

She didna comb her yellow hair,
  Nor make meikle o' her head ;
And ilka thing that lady took,
  Was like to be her deid.

It's four and twenty ladies fair
  Were playing at the ba' ;
Janet, the brightest of them anes,
  Was faintest o' them a'.

Four and twenty ladies fair
  Were playing at the chess ;
And out there came the fair Janet,
  As green as any grass.

Out and spak an old grey-headed knight
  Lay o'er the castle wa'—
"And ever, alas ! for thee, Janet,
  But we'll be blamed a' !"

"Now haud your tongue, ye auld grey knight !
  And an ill deid may ye die,
Father my bairn on whom I will
  I'll father nane on thee."

446

Out then spake her father dear,
  And he spake meek and mild—
"And ever, alas! my sweet Janet,
  I fear ye gae with child."

"And if I be with child, father,
  Mysell maun bear the blame;
There's ne'er a knight about your ha'
  Shall hae the bairnie's name.

"And if I be with child, father,
  'Twill prove a wondrous birth,
For weel I swear I'm not wi' bairn
  To any man on earth.

"If my love were an earthly knight,
  As he's an elfin grey,
I wadna gie my ain true love
  For nae lord that ye hae."

She prink'd hersell and prinn'd hersell,
  By the ae light o' the moon,
And she's away to Carterhaugh,
  To speak wi' young Tamlane.

And when she came to Carterhaugh,
  She gaed beside the well;
But there she saw the steed standing,
  But away was himsell.

She hadna pu'd a double rose,
  A rose but only twae,
When up and started young Tamlane,
  Says—"Lady, thou pu's nae mae!

" Why pu' ye the rose, Janet,
  Within this garden grene,
And a' to kill the bonny babe,
  That we got us between ? "

" The truth ye'll tell to me, Tamlane,
  A word ye mauna lie ;
Gin e'er ye was in haly chapel,
  Or sained in Christentie ? "—

" The truth I'll tell to thee, Janet,
  A word I winna lie ;
A knight me got, and a lady me bore,
  As well as they did thee.

" Randolph, Earl Murray, was my sire,
  Dunbar, Earl March, is thine ;
We loved when we were children small,
  Which yet you well may mind.

" When I was a boy just turn'd of nine,
  My uncle sent for me,
To hunt, and hawk, and ride with him,
  And keep him companie.

" There came a wind out of the north,
  A sharp wind and a snell ;
And a deep sleep came over me,
  And frae my horse I fell.

" The Queen of Fairies keepit me,
  In yon green hill to dwell ;
And I'm a fairy, lyth and limb ;
  Fair lady, view me well.

" But we, that live in Fairyland,
   No sickness know, nor pain ;
I quit my body when I will,
   And take to it again.

" I quit my body when I please,
   Or unto it repair ;
We can inhabit, at our ease,
   In either earth or air.

" Our shapes and size we can convert
   To either large or small ;
An old nutshell's the same to us
   As is the lofty hall.

" We sleep in rose-buds soft and sweet,
   We revel in the stream ;
We wanton lightly on the wind,
   Or glide on a sunbeam.

" And all our wants are well supplied
   From every rich man's store,
Who thankless sins the gifts he gets,
   And vainly grasps for more.

" Then would I never tire, Janet,
   In elfish land to dwell ;
But aye, at every seven years,
   They pay the teind to hell ;
And I'm sae fat and fair of flesh,
   I fear 'twill be mysell.

" This night is Hallowe'en, Janet,
　The morn is Hallowday ;
And, gin ye dare your true love win,
　Ye hae nae time to stay.

" The night it is good Hallowe'en,
　When fairy folk will ride ;
And they that wad their true love win,
　At Miles Cross they maun bide."—

" But how shall I thee ken, Tamlane?
　Or how shall I thee knaw,
Amang so many unearthly knights,
　The like I never saw? "—

" The first company that passes by.
　Say na, and let them gae ;
The next company that passes by,
　Say na, and do right sae ;
The third company that passes by,
　Then I'll be ane o' thae.

" First, let pass the black, Janet,
　And syne let pass the brown ;
But grip ye to the milk-white steed,
　And pu' the rider down.

" For I ride on the milk-white steed,
　And aye nearest the town ;
Because I was a christen'd knight,
　They gave me that renown.

" My right hand will be gloved, Janet,
　My left hand will be bare ;
And these the tokens I gie thee,
　Nae doubt I will be there.

" They'll turn me in your arms, Janet,
    An adder and a snake,
But haud me fast, let me not pass,
    Gin ye would buy me maik.

" They'll turn me in your arms, Janet,
    An adder and an ask ;
They'll turn me in your arms, Janet,
    A bale that burns fast.

" They'll turn me in your arms, Janet,
    A red-hot gad o' airn ;
But haud me fast, let me not pass,
    For I'll do you no harm.

" First dip me in a stand o' milk,
    And then in a stand o' water ;
But haud me fast, let me not pass—
    I'll be your bairn's father.

"And, next, they'll shape me in your arms
    A tod, but and an eel ;
But haud me fast, nor let me gang,
    As you do love me weel.

" They'll shape me in your arms, Janet,
    A dove, but and a swan ;
And last they'll shape me in your arms
    A mother-naked man :
Cast your green mantle over me—
    I'll be myself again."—

Gloomy, gloomy was the night,
   And eiry was the way,
As fair Janet, in her green mantle,
   To Miles Cross she did gae.

The heavens were black, the night was dark,
   And dreary was the place ;
But Janet stood, with eager wish,
   Her lover to embrace.

Betwixt the hours of twelve and one,
   A north wind tore the bent ;
And she heard strange elritch sounds
   Upon that wind which went.

About the dead hour o' the night
   She heard the bridles ring ;
And Janet was as glad o' that
   As any earthly thing.

Their oaten pipes blew wondrous shrill,
   The hemlock small blew clear ;
And louder notes from hemlock large,
   And bog-reed, struck the ear ;
But solemn sounds, or sober thoughts,
   The Fairies cannot bear.

They sing, inspired with love and joy,
   Like skylarks in the air ;
Of solid sense, or thought that's grave,
   You'll find no traces there.

Fair Janet stood, with mind unmoved,
   The dreary heath upon ;
And louder, louder wax'd the sound,
   As they came riding on.

Will o'-Wisp before them went,
　Sent forth a twinkling light;
And soon she saw the Fairy bands
　All riding in her sight.

And first gaed by the black, black steed,
　And then gaed by the brown;
And fast she gript the milk-white steed,
　And pu'd the rider down.

She pu'd him frae the milk-white steed,
　And loot the bridle fa';
And up there raise an erlish cry—
　"He's wan among us a'!"—

They shaped him in fair Janet's arms
　An esk, but and an adder;
She held him fast in every shape—
　To be her bairn's father.

They shaped him in her arms at last
　A mother-naked man:
She wrapp'd him in her green mantle,
　And sae her lover wan!

Up then spake the Queen o' Fairies,
　Out o' a bush o' broom—
"She that has borrow'd young Tamlane,
　Has gotten a stately groom."—

Up then spake the Queen o' Fairies,
　Out o' a bush o' rye—
"She's ta'en away the bonniest knight
　In a' my companie.

"But had I kenn'd, Tamlane," she says,
  "A lady wad borrow'd thee—
I wad ta'en out thy twa grey e'en,
  Put in twa e'en o' tree.

"Had I but kenn'd, Tamlane," she says,
  "Before ye came frae hame—
I wad ta'en out your heart o' flesh,
  Put in a heart o' stane.

"Had I but had the wit yestreen
  That I hae coft the day—
I'd paid my kanes seven times to hell
  Ere you'd been won away!"

OLD BALLAD.

THE BROWNIE OF BLEDNOCH.

THERE came a strange wight to our town-en',
An' the fient a body did him ken ;
He tirled na lang, but he glided ben
    Wi' a dreary, dreary hum.

His face did glow like the glow o' the west,
When the drumly cloud has it half o'ercast ;
Or the struggling moon when she's sair distrest,
    O sirs, 'twas Aiken-drum.

I trow the bauldest stood aback,
Wi' a gape an' a glower till their lugs did crack,
As the shapeless phantom mum'ling spak—
    "Hae ye wark for Aiken-drum!"

Oh, had ye seen the bairns's fright,
As they stared at this wild and unyirthly wight;
As they skulkit in 'tween the dark and the light,
    And graned out, "Aiken-drum!"

The black dog, growling, cowered his tail,
The lassie swarfed, loot fa' the pail;
Rob's lingle brak as he mendit the flail,
    At the sight o' Aiken-drum.

His matted head on his breast did rest,
A lang blue beard wan'ered down like a vest;
But the glare o' his ee hath nae bard exprest,
    Nor the skimes o' Aiken-drum.

Roun' his hairy form there was naething seen
But a philabeg o' the rashes green,
An' his knotted knees played aye knoit between—
    What a sight was Aiken-drum!

On his wauchie arms three claws did meet,
As they trailed on the grun' by his taeless feet;
E'en the old gudeman himsel' did sweat
    To look at Aiken-drum.

But he drew a score, himsel' did sain;
The auld wife tried, but her tongue was gane;
While the young one closer clasped her wean,
    And turned frae Aiken-drum.

But the canty auld wife cam till her breath,
And she thocht the Bible might ward aff scaith,
Be it benshee, bogle, ghaist, or wraith—
    But it feared na Aiken-drum.

" His presence protect us ! " quoth the old gudeman ;
" What wad ye, whare won ye, by sea or by lan' ?
I conjure ye, speak, by the beuk in my han' ! "
  What a grane gae Aiken-drum !

" I lived in a lan' where we saw nae sky,
I dwelt in a spot where a burn rins na by ;
But I'se dwall now wi' you if ye like to try—
  Hae ye wark for Aiken-drum ?

" I'll shiel a' your sheep i' the mornin' sune,
I'll berry your crap by the light o' the moon,
An' ba the bairns wi' an unkenned tune,
  If ye'll keep puir Aiken-drum.

" I'll loup the linn where ye canna wade,
I'll kirn the kirn, an' I'll turn the bread ;
An' the wildest filly that ever ran rede,
  I'se tame't," quoth Aiken-drum.

" To wear the tod frae the flock on the fell,
To gather the dew frae the heather-bell,
An' to look at my face i' your clear crystal well,
  Might gie pleasure to Aiken-drum.

" I'se seek nae guids, gear, bond, nor mark ;
I use nae beddin', shoon, nor sark ;
But a cogfu' o' brose 'tween the light an' the dark,
  Is the wage o' Aiken-drum."

Quoth the wylie auld wife : " The thing speaks weel ;
Our workers are scant—we hae routh o' meal ;
Gif he'll do as he says—be he man, be he deil—
  Now ! we'll try this Aiken-drum."

But the wenches skirled : "He's no be here !
His eldritch look gars us swarf wi' fear ;
An' the feint a ane will the house come near,
    If they think but o' Aiken-drum."

" Puir clipmalabors ! ye hae little wit ;
Is't na Hallowmas now, an' the crap out yet ? "
Sae she silenced them a' wi' a stamp o' her fit—
    " Sit yer wa's down, Aiken-drum."

. Roun' a' that side what wark was dune
By the streamer's gleam, or the glance o' the moon ;
A word, or a wish, an' the brownie cam sune,
    Sae helpfu' was Aiken-drum. .   .   .

On Blednoch banks, an' on crystal Cree,
For mony a day a toiled wight was he ;
While the bairns played harmless roun' his knee,
    Sae social was Aiken-drum.

But a new-made wife, fu' o' frippish freaks,
Fond o' a' things feat for the first five weeks,
Laid a mouldy pair o' her ain man's breeks
    By the brose o' Aiken-drum.

Let the learned decide when they convene
What spell was him an' the breeks between ;
For frae that day forth he was nae mair seen,
    An' sair missed was Aiken-drum.

He was heard by a herd gaun by Thrieve,
Crying : " Lang, lang now may I greet an' grieve :
For, alas ! I hae gotten baith fee an' leave—
    Oh, luckless Aiken-drum."

Awa', ye wrangling sceptic tribe,
Wi' your pros an' your cons wad ye decide
'Gain the 'sponsible voice o' a hail country-side,
    On the facts 'bout Aiken-drum !

Though the " Brownie o' Blednoch " lang be gane,
The mark o' his feet's left on mony a stane ;
An' mony a wife an' mony a wean
    Tell the feats o' Aiken-drum.

E'en now, light loons that jibe an' sneer
At spiritual guests an' a' sic gear,
At the Glashnoch mill hae swat wi' fear,
    An' looked roun' for Aiken-drum.

An' guidly folks hae gotten a fright,
When the moon was set, an' the stars gied nae light,
At the roaring linn, in the howe o' the night,
    Wi' sighs like Aiken-drum.

               WILLIAM NICHOLSON.

LA BELLE DAME SANS MERCI.

I.

AH, what can ail thee wretched wight,
  Alone and palely loitering ;
The sedge is wither'd from the lake,
  And no birds sing.

II.

Ah, what can ail thee, wretched wight.
  So haggard and so woe-begone ?
The squirrel's granary is full
  And the harvest's done.

III.

I see a lily on thy brow,
  With anguish moist and fever dew ;
And on thy cheek a fading rose
  Fast withereth too.

IV.

I met a lady in the meads,
  Full beautiful, a faery's child ;
Her hair was long, her foot was light,
  And her eyes were wild.

V.

I set her on my pacing steed,
  And nothing else saw all day long ;
For sideways would she lean, and sing
  A faery's song.

VI.

I made a garland for her head,
  And bracelets too, and fragrant zone ;
She look'd at me as she did love,
  And made sweet moan.

VII.

She found me roots of relish sweet,
  And honey wild, and manna dew ;
And sure in language strange she said,
  I love thee true.

VIII.

She took me to her elfin grot,
  And there she gaz'd and sighed deep,
And there I shut her wild sad eyes—
  So kiss'd to sleep.

IX.

And there we slumber'd on the moss,
  And there I dream'd, ah woe betide,
The latest dream I ever dream'd
  On the cold hill-side.

X.

I saw pale kings, and princes too,
  Pale warriors, death-pale were they all ;
Who cry'd—'' La belle Dame sans merci
  Hath thee in thrall ! ''

XI.

I saw their starv'd lips in the gloom
  With horrid warning gaped wide,
And I awoke, and found me here
  On the cold hill-side.

XII.

And this is why I sojourn here
  Alone and palely loitering,
Though the sedge is wither'd from the lake,
  And no birds sing.

JOHN KEATS.

THE MOUNTAIN SPRITE.

IN yonder valley there dwelt, alone,
A youth, whose moments had calmly flown,
Till spells came o'er him, and, day and night,
He was haunted and watched by a Mountain Sprite !

As once, by moonlight, he wandered o'er
The golden sands of that island shore,
A foot-print sparkled before his sight—
'Twas the fairy foot of the Mountain Sprite !

Beside a fountain, one sunny day,
As bending over the stream he lay,
There peep'd down o'er him two eyes of light,
And he saw in that mirror the Mountain Sprite.

He turn'd, but lo, like a startled bird,
That spirit fled !—and the youth but heard
Sweet music, such as marks the flight
Of some bird of song, from the Mountain Sprite.

One night, still haunted by that bright look,
The boy, bewilder'd, his pencil took,
And, guided only by memory's light,
Drew the once-seen form of the Mountain Sprite.

"Oh thou, who lovest the shadow," cried
A voice, low whisp'ring by his side,
"Now turn and see,"—here the youth's delight
Seal'd the rosy lips of the Mountain Sprite.

"Of all the Spirits of land and sea,"
Then rapt he murmur'd, "there's none like thee,
And oft, oh oft, may thy foot thus light
In this lonely bower, sweet Mountain Sprite!"

THOMAS MOORE.

THE FAIRY BOY.

A MOTHER came when stars were paling,
    Wailing round a lonely spring;
Thus she cried while tears were falling,
    Calling on the Fairy King:

"Why with spells my child caressing,
    Courting him with fairy joy;
Why destroy a mother's blessing,
    Wherefore steal my baby boy?

"O'er the mountain, through the wild wood,
    Where his childhood loved to play;
Where the flowers are freshly springing,
    There I wander, day by day.

447

"There I wander, growing fonder
   Of the child that made my joy ;
On the echoes wildly calling
   To restore my fairy boy.

"But in vain my plaintive calling
   Tears are falling all in vain !
He now sports with fairy pleasure,
   He's the treasure of their train !

"Fare thee well, my child, for ever,
   In this world I've lost my joy,
But in the *next* we ne'er shall sever,
   There I'll find my angel boy ! "

SAMUEL LOVER.

THE FAIRY TEMPTER.

A FAIR girl was sitting in the greenwood shade,
List'ning to the music the spring birds made ;
When sweeter by far than the birds on the tree,
A voice murmur'd near her, "Oh come, love, with me —
      In earth or air,
      A thing so fair
      I have not seen as thee !
   Then come, love, with me."

"With a star for thy home, in a palace of light,
Thou wilt add a fresh grace to the beauty of night ;
Or, if wealth be thy wish, thine are treasures untold,
I will show thee the birthplace of jewels and gold—
      And pearly caves
      Beneath the waves,
      All these, all these are thine,
   If thou wilt be mine."

Thus whisper'd a fairy to tempt the fair girl,
But vain was his promise of gold and of pearl ;
For she said, ''Tho' thy gifts to a poor girl were dear,
My father, my mother, my sisters are here :
　　　Oh ! what would be
　　　Thy gifts to me
　　　Of earth, and sea, and air,
If my heart were not there ? ''

　　　　　　　SAMUEL LOVER.

THE FAIRIES OF THE CALDON-LOW.

A MIDSUMMER LEGEND.

'' AND where have you been, my Mary,
　　And where have you been from me ? ''
'' I've been to the top of the Caldon-Low,
　　The midsummer night to see ! ''

'' And what did you see, my Mary,
　　All up on the Caldon-Low ? ''
'' I saw the blithe sunshine come down,
　　And I saw the merry winds blow.''

'' And what did you hear, my Mary,
　　All up on the Caldon-Hill ? ''
'' I heard the drops of the water made,
　　And the green corn ears to fill.''

'' Oh, tell me all, my Mary—
　　All, all that ever you know ;
For you must have seen the fairies,
　　Last night on the Caldon-Low.''

"Then take me on your knee, mother,
　And listen, mother of mine :
A hundred fairies danced last night,
　And the harpers they were nine.

"And merry was the glee of the harp-strings,
　And their dancing feet so small ;
But, oh, the sound of their talking
　Was merrier far than all !"

"And what were the words, my Mary,
　That you did hear them say ? "
"I'll tell you all, my mother—
　But let me have my way !

"And some they played with the water,
　And rolled it down the hill ;
'And this,' they said, ' shall speedily turn
　The poor old miller's mill ;

"'For there has been no water,
　Ever since the first of May ;
And a busy man shall the miller be
　By the dawning of the day !

"'Oh, the miller, how he will laugh,
　When he sees the mill-dam rise !
The jolly old miller, how he will laugh,
　Till the tears fill both his eyes ! '

"And some they seized the little winds,
　That sounded over the hill,
And each put a horn into his mouth,
　And blew so sharp and shrill :—

" 'And there,' said they, 'the merry winds go,
　Away from every horn ;
And those shall clear the mildew dank
　From the blind old widow's corn.

" ' Oh, the poor blind old widow—
　Though she has been blind so long,
She'll be merry enough when the mildew's gone,
　And the corn stands stiff and strong.'

"And some they brought the brown lintseed,
　And flung it down from the Low—
' And this,' said they, ' by the sunrise,
　In the weaver's croft shall grow !

" 'Oh, the poor, lame weaver,
　How will he laugh outright,
When he sees his dwindling flax-field
　All full of flowers by night !'

"And then upspoke a brownie,
　With a long beard on his chin—
' I have spun up all the tow,' said he,
　' And I want some more to spin.

" ' I've spun a piece of hempen cloth,
　And I want to spin another—
A little sheet for Mary's bed,
　And an apron for her mother !'

"And with that I could not help but laugh,
　And I laughed out loud and free :
And then on the top of the Caldon-Low,
　There was no one left but me.

"And all, on the top of the Caldon-Low,
    The mists were cold and grey,
And nothing I saw but the mossy stones
    That round about me lay.

" But, as I came down from the hill-top,
    I heard, afar below,
How busy the jolly miller was,
    And how merry the wheel did go.

"And I peeped into the widow's field ;
    And, sure enough, was seen
The yellow ears of the mildewed corn
    All standing stiff and green.

" And down by the weaver's cot I stole,
    To see if the flax were high ;
But I saw the weaver at his gate,
    With the good news in his eye !

" Now, this is all I heard, mother,
    And all that I did see ;
So, prithee, make my bed, mother,
    For I'm tired as I can be."
                            MARY HOWITT.

THE FAIRIES' PASSAGE.

I.

TAPP, tapp ! Rapp, rapp ! "Get up, Gaffer Ferry-
    man."
    " Eh ? who is there ? "   The clock strikes Three.
"Get up, do, Gaffer !   You are the very man
    We have been long—long—longing to see."

The ferryman rises, growling and grumbling,
And goes fum-fumbling, and stumbling, and tumbling,
Over the wares in his way to the door.
    But he secs no more
    Than he saw before,
Till a voice is heard—" O Ferryman, dear !
Here we are waiting, all of us here !
We are a wee, wee colony, we ;
Some two hundred in all, or three.
Ferry us over the river Lee
    Ere dawn of day,
    And we will pay
    The most we may,
    In our own wee way ! "

II.

" Who are you ? Whence came you ? What place are
  you going to ? "
" O, we have dwelt over-long in this land.
The people get cross, and are growing so knowing, too ;
 Nothing at all but they now understand ;
We are daily vanishing under the thunder
Of some huge engine or iron wonder ;
 That iron—O, it has entered our souls ! "
    "——Your souls ? O, Goles !
    You queer little drolls ! [speed,
Do you mean——? " " Good Gaffer, do aid us with
For our time, like our stature, is short indeed !
And a very long way we have to go,
Eight or ten thousand miles or so, .
Hither and thither, and to and fro ;
    With our pots and pans,
    And little gold cans ;
    But our light caravans
    Run swifter than man's ! "

III.

"Well, well, you may come !" said the Ferryman,
    affably ;
"Patrick, turn out, and get ready the barge !"
Then again to the little folk—"Though you seem laugh-
    ably
    Small, I don't mind, if your coppers be large."
O, dear ! what a rushing, what pushing, what crushing
(The waterman making vain efforts at hushing
    The hubbub the while) there followed these words !
        What clapping of boards !
        What strapping of cords !
    What stowing away of children and wives,
    And platters, and mugs, and spoons, and knives !
    Till all had safely got into the boat,
    And the Ferryman clad in his tip-top coat,
    And his wee little fairies were fairly afloat !
        Then ding ! ding ! ding !
        And kling ! kling ! kling !
        How the coppers did ring
        In the tin pitcherling !

IV.

Off, then, went the boat, at first very pleasantly,
    Smoothly, and so forth, but after a while
It swayed and it swagged this way and that way, and
    presently
    Chest after chest, and pile after pile,
Of the little folks' goods began tossing and rolling,
And pitching like fun, beyond fairy controlling !
    O, Mab ! if the hubbub was great before,
    It was now some two or three million times more ;
    Crash went the wee crocks, and the clocks, and the
    locks,

Of each little wee box were stove in by hard knocks;
And then there were oaths, and prayers, and cries—
"Take care!"—"See there!"—"Oh, dear! my
    eyes!"
"I am killed!"—"I am drowned!"-- with groans
    and sighs;
            Till to land they drew;
            " Yeo hoe! Pull to!
            Tiller-rope, thro' and thro'!"
            And all's right anew.

v.

"Now, jump upon shore, ye queer little oddities,
   . . . Eh! what is this? . Where are they at all?
Where are they and where are their tiny commodities?
   Well! as I live!" He looks blank as a wall,
    The poor Ferryman! Round him, and round him
      he gazes,
    But only gets deeplier lost in the mazes
    Of utter bewilderment! All, all are gone—
          And he stands alone,
          Like a statue of stone,
    In a doldrum of wonder. He turns to steer,
    And a tinkling laugh salutes his ear
    With other odd sounds—" Ha! ha! ha! ha!
    Tol, lol; zid, ziddle—quee, quee—bah! bah!
    Fizzigigiggidy! phse! sha! sha!"
"O, ye thieves, ye thieves! ye rascally thieves!"
   The good man cries. He turns to his pitcher,
And there, alas! to his horror perceives,
   That the little folks' mode of making him richer
Had been to pay with him—withered leaves!

                  CLARENCE MANGAN·

THUBBER-NA-SHIE;

OR, THE FAIRY WELL.

[Amongst the many old and fanciful superstitions embodied in the traditions of our peasantry, some of the most poetical are those connected with spring wells, which in Ireland have been invested with something of a sacred character ever since the days of Druidical worship. It is in some parts of the country an article of popular belief, that the desecration of a spring by any unworthy use is followed invariably by some misfortune to the offender; and that the well itself, which is regarded as the source of fruitfulness and prosperity, moves altogether out of the fields in which the violation has been committed.—*Dublin University Magazine*, vol. viii., p. 449.]

OH ! Peggy Bawn was innocent,
  And wild as any roe ;
Her cheek was like the summer rose,
  Her neck was like the snow :

And every eye was in her head
  So beautiful and bright,
You'd almost think they'd light her through
  Glencarrigy by night.

Among the hills and mountains,
  Above her mother's home,
The long and weary summer day
  Young Peggy Blake would roam ;

And not a girl in all the town,
  From Dhua to Glenlur,
Could wander through the mountain's heath
  Or climb the rocks with her.

The Lammas sun was shinin' on
   The meadows all so brown ;
The neighbours gathered far and near
   To cut the ripe crops down ;

And pleasant was the mornin',
   And dewy was the dawn,
And gay and lightsome-hearted
   To the sunny fields they're gone.

The joke was passing lightly,
   And the laugh was loud and free ;
There was neither care nor trouble
   To disturb their hearty glee ;

When, says Peggy, resting in among
   The sweet and scented hay,
" I wonder is there one would brave
   The Fairy-well to-day !"

She looked up with her laughin' eyes,
   So soft at Willy Rhu ;
Och murdher ! that she didn't need
   His warnin' kind and true !

But all the boys and girls laughed,
   And Willy Rhu looked shy ;
God help you, Willy ! sure they saw
   The throuble in your eye.

" Now, by my faith !" young Connell says—
   " I like your notion well—
There's a power more than gospel
   In what crazy gossips tell."

Oh, my heavy hatred fall upon
   Young Connell of Sliabh-Mast !
IIe took the cruel vengeance
   For his scorned love at last.

The jokin' and the jibin'
   And the banterin' went on,
One girl dared another,
   And they all dared Peggy Bawn.

Till, leaping up, away she flew
   Down to the hollow green—
Her bright locks, floating in the wind,
   Like golden lights were seen.

They saw her at the Fairy-well—
   Their laughin' died away,
They saw her stoop above its brink
   With heart as cold as clay.

Oh ! mother, mother, never stand
   Upon your cabin floor !
You heard the cry that through your heart
   Will ring for evermore ;

For when she came up from the well,
   No one could stand her look :
Her eye was wild—her cheek was pale—
   They saw her mind was shook :

And the gaze she cast around her
   Was so ghastly and so sad—
"O Christ preserve us !" shouted all,
   " Poor Peggy Blake's gone mad !"

The moon was up—the stars were out,
  And shining through the sky,
When young and old stood mourning round
  To see their darling die.

Poor Peggy from her death-bed rose—
  Her face was pale and cold,
And down about her shoulders hung
  The lovely locks of gold.

"All you that's here this night," she said,
  "Take warnin' by my fate,
Whoever braves the Fairies' wrath,
  Their sorrow comes too late."

The tear was startin' in her eye,
  She clasp'd her throbbin' head,
And when the sun next mornin' rose
  Poor Peggy Bawn was dead.

JAMES TEELING.

THE HAUNTED SPRING.

[It is said, Fays have the power to assume various shapes for the purpose of luring mortals into Fairyland; hunters seem to have been particularly the objects of the lady fairies' fancies.]

GAILY through the mountain glen
  The hunter's horn did ring,
    As the milk-white doe
    Escaped his bow,
  Down by the haunted spring.
In vain his silver horn he wound,—
  'Twas echo answered back ;
For neither groom nor baying hound
  Were on the hunter's track

In vain he sought the milk-white doe
That made him stray, and 'scaped his bow;
For, save himself, no living thing
Was by the silent haunted spring.

The purple heath-bells, blooming fair,
    Their fragrance round did fling,
        As the hunter lay
        At close of day,
    Down by the haunted spring.
A lady fair, in robe of white,
    To greet the hunter came;
She kissed a cup with jewels bright,
    And pledged him by his name;
" Oh, lady fair," the hunter cried,
" Be thou my love, my blooming bride,
A bride that well may grace a king !
Fair lady of the haunted spring."

In the fountain clear she stoop'd,
    And forth she drew a ring;
        And that loved Knight
        His faith did plight
    Down by the haunted spring.
But since that day his chase did stray,
    The hunter ne'er was seen,
And legends tell, he now doth dwell
    Within the hills so green ;*
But still the milk-white doe appears,
And wakes the peasants' evening fears,
While distant bugles faintly ring
Around the lonely haunted spring.

                    SAMUEL LOVER.

* Fays and fairies are supposed to have their dwelling-places
within old green hills.

THE ROMANCE OF THE FAIRY CURE.

I.

Nelly Phelan's child is ailing ;
Hour by hour, the babe is failing ;
Squeeling, kicking, biting, whining,
To an atomy he's pining.

II.

Once he was a fine, wee fellow ;
Now he's wrinkled, thin, and yellow.
Playful then he was, and civil ;
Now he's cross-grained, as the devil.

III.

To a wise woman Nell's walking ;
Long time they're in secret talking ;
First she heard all Nell's description ;
Then she wrote out a prescription.

IV.

" Take this cure, although a strange one ;
It is needed when they change one ;
By it you'll the fairies bother,
Get your child, and choke the other.

V.

" You must make the fairy speak out,
Ere your child, from them, you take out.
If you follow what's here written,
You shall find the biter bitten."

VI.

Cried Nell, " Be sure that I'll observe it ;
If I fail I'll not deserve it :
I would walk the wide world over,
If my child I could recover."

VII.

Five hundred egg-shells Nelly chooses
In a pot, the shells she bruises ;
In spring water now they're boiling,
Stirring round the pot she's toiling.

VIII.

Red-hot now the poker's ready ;
While Nell stirs the pot, so steady :
From the child, in cradle lying,
Nell now hears a strange voice crying--

IX.

" Mammy ! Mammy ! what's that boiling ?
Why with potstick are you toiling ? "
Nell, with fright, to drop was ready,
Yet she answered, cool, and steady—

X.

" Egg-shells, deary ! I am brewing,
Cock's broth for my babe I'm stewing.
When I skim off all the dripping,
Then it will be fit for sipping."

XI.

"Though five hundred years I'm chewing,
Egg-shells never saw I brewing;
Though five centuries I'm cheating,
Ne'er have I seen cock's broth eating."

XII.

Quick the poker Nelly seizes;
To the cradle now she races;
Red-hot down its throat she crams it;
With her might and main she rams it.

XIII.

Gone like lightning is the fairy;
In its stead, there lies her deary—
Her brave boy—her darling Terry,
With his lip and cheek of cherry.

JAMES CLARENCE MANGAN.

THE FAIRY NURSE.

SWEET babe! a golden cradle holds thee,
And soft the snow-white fleece enfolds thee;
In airy bower I'll watch thy sleeping.
Where branchy trees to the breeze are sweeping.
Shuheen, sho, lulo lo!

When mothers languish broken-hearted,
When young wives are from husbands parted,
Ah! little think the keeners lonely,
They weep some time-worn fairy only.
                    Shuheen, sho, lulo lo!

Within our magic halls of brightness,
Trips many a foot of snowy whiteness;
Stolen maidens, queens of fairy—
And kings and chiefs a sluagh shee airy.
                    Shuheen, sho, lulo lo!

Rest thee, babe! I love thee dearly,
And as thy mortal mother nearly;
Ours is the swiftest steed and proudest,
That moves where the tramp of the host is loudest.
                    Shuheen, sho, lulo lo!

Rest, thee, babe! for soon thy slumbers
Shall flee at the magic Koelshie's numbers;
In airy bower I'll watch thy sleeping,
Where branchy trees to the breeze are sweeping.
                    Shuheen, sho, lulo lo!

                              EDWARD WALSH.

THE FAIRY THORN.

AN ULSTER BALLAD.

"Get up, our Anna dear, from the weary spinning
        wheel;
  For your father's on the hill, and your mother is asleep:
Come up above the crags, and we'll dance a highland reel
  Around the fairy thorn on the steep."

At Anna Grace's door 'twas thus the maidens cried,
    Three merry maidens fair in kirtles of the green ;
And Anna laid the rock and the weary wheel aside,
    The fairest of the four, I ween.

They're glancing through the glimmer of the quiet eve,
    Away in milky wavings of the neck and ankle bare ;
The merry-sliding stream in its sleepy song they leave,
    And the crags in the ghostly air :

And linking hand and hand, and singing as they go,
    The maids along the hill-side have ta'en their fearless
        way
Till they come to where the rowan trees in lonely beauty
        grow
    Beside the Fairy Hawthorn grey.

The Hawthorn stands between the ashes tall and slim,
    Like matron with her twin grand-daughters at her knee;
The rowan berries cluster o'er her low head grey and dim,
    In ruddy kisses sweet to see.

The merry maidens four have ranged them in a row,
    Between each lovely couple a stately rowan stem,
And away in mazes wavy like skimming birds they go,
    Oh, never carolled bird like them !

But solemn is the silence of the silvery haze
    That drinks away their voices in echoless repose,
And dreamily the evening has stilled the haunted braes,
    And dreamier the gloaming grows.

And sinking one by one, like lark-notes from the sky
    When the falcon's shadow saileth across the open shaw,
Are hushed the maidens' voices, as cowering down they
        lie
    In the flutter of their sudden awe.

For, from the air above, and the grassy ground beneath,
   And from the mountain-ashes and the old whitethorn
      between,
A power of fa¡nt enchantment doth through their beings
      breathe
   And they sink down together on the green.

They sink together silent, and stealing side by side,
   They fling their lovely arms o'er their drooping necks
      so fair,
Then vainly strive again their naked arms to hide,
   For their shrinking necks again are bare.

Thus clasped and prostrate all, with their heads together
      bowed,
   Soft o'er their bosoms beating—the only human sound—
They hear the silky footsteps of the silent fairy crowd,
   Like a river in the air, gliding round.

Nor scream can any raise, nor prayer can any say,
   But wild, wild the terror of the speechless three—
For they feel fair Anna Grace drawn silently away,
   By whom they dare not look to see.

They feel their tresses twine with her parting locks of
      gold,
   And the curls elastic falling, as her head withdraws ;
They feel her sliding arms from their tranced arms unfold,
   But they dare not look to see the cause :

For heavy on their senses the faint enchantment lies
   Through all that night of anguish and perilous amaze ;
And neither fear nor wonder can ope their quivering eyes
   Or their limbs from the cold ground raise.

Till out of Night the earth has rolled her dewy side,
  With every haunted mountain and streamy vale below ;
When, as the mist dissolves in the yellow morning tide,
  The maidens' trance dissolveth so.

Then fly the ghastly three as swiftly as they may,
  And told their tale of sorrow to anxious friends in vain—
They pined away and died within the year and day,
  And ne'er was Anna Grace seen again.

Samuel Ferguson, M.R.I.A.

THE FAIRY WELL OF LAGNANAY.

I.

Mournfully, sing mournfully—
  "O listen, Ellen, sister dear ;
Is there no help at all for me,
    But only ceaseless sigh and tear ?
    Why did not he who left me here,
With stolen hope steal memory ?
    O listen, Ellen, sister dear,
(Mournfully, sing mournfully)—
    I'll go away to Sleamish hill,
I'll pluck the fairy hawthorne tree,
    And let the spirits work their will ;
    I care not if for good or ill,
So they but lay the memory
    Which all my heart is haunting still !
(Mournfully, sing mournfully)—
    The Fairies are a silent race,
And pale as lily flowers to see ;
    I care not for a blanched face,

Nor wandering in a dreaming place,
So I but banish memory :—
　I wish I were with Anna Grace !"
Mournfully, sing mournfully !—

II.

Hearken to my tale of woe—
　'Twas thus to weeping Ellen Con,
Her sister said in accents low,
　Her only sister, Una bawn :
　'Twas in their bed before the dawn,
And Ellen answered sad and slow,—
　" Oh Una, Una, be not drawn
(Hearken to my tale of woe)—
　To this unholy grief I pray,
Which makes me sick at heart to know,
　And I will help you if I may :
　—The Fairy Well of Lagnanay—
Lie nearer me, I tremble so,—
　Una, I've heard wise women say
(Hearken to my tale of woe)—
　That if before the dews arise,
True maiden in its icy flow
　With pure hand bathe her bosom thrice,
　Three lady-brackens pluck likewise,
And three times round the fountain go,
　She straight forgets her tears and sighs."
Hearken to my tale of woe !

III.

All, alas ! and well-away !
　" Oh, sister Ellen, sister sweet,
Come with me to the hill I pray,
　And I will prove that blessed freet ! "
They rose with soft and silent feet,

They left their mother where she lay,
　Their mother and her care discreet,
(All, alas ! and well-away !)
　And soon they reached the Fairy Well,
The mountain's eye, clear, cold, and grey,
　Wide open in the dreary fell :
　How long they stood 'twere vain to tell,
At last upon the point of day,
　Bawn Una bares her bosom's swell,
　(All, alas ! and well-away !)
　Thrice o'er her shrinking breasts she laves
The gliding glance that will not stay
　Of subtly-streaming fairy waves :—
　And now the charm three brackens craves,
She plucks them in their fringed array :—
　Now round the well her fate she braves,
(All, alas ! and well-away !)

IV.

Save us all from Fairy thrall !
　Ellen sees her face the rim
Twice and thrice, and that is all—
　Fount and hill and maiden swim,
　All together melting dim !
"Una ! Una !" thou may'st call,
　Sister sad ! but lith or limb
(Save us all from Fairy thrall !)
　Never again of Una bawn
Where now she walks in dreamy hall
　Shall eye of mortal look upon !
　Oh ! can it be the guard was gone,
That better guard than shield or wall ?
　Who knows on earth save Turlagh Daune ?

(Save us all from Fairy thrall !)
  Behold the banks are green and bare,
No pit is here wherein to fall :
  Aye—at the fount you well may stare,
  But nought save pebbles smooth is there,
And small streams twirling one and all.
  Hie thee home, and be thy pray'r,
Save us all from Fairy thrall !

SAMUEL FERGUSON, LL.D., M.R.I.A.

THE KELPIE OF CORRIEVRECKAN.

I.

HE mounted his steed of the water clear,
And sat on his saddle of sea-weed sere ;
He held his bridle of strings of pearl,
Dug out of the depths where the sea-snakes curl.

II.

He put on his vest of the whirlpool froth,
Soft and dainty as velvet cloth,
And donn'd his mantle of sand so white,
And grasp'd his sword of the coral bright.

III.

And away he gallop'd, a horseman free,
Spurring his steed through the stormy sea,
Clearing the billows with bound and leap—
Away, away, o'er the foaming deep !

IV.

By Scarba's rock, by Lunga's shore,
By Garveloch isles where the breakers roar,
With his horse's hoofs he dash'd the spray,
And on to Loch Buy, away, away !

V.

On to Loch Buy all day he rode,
And reach'd the shore as sunset glow'd,
And stopp'd to hear the sounds of joy
That rose from the hills and glens of Moy.

VI.

The morrow was May, and on the green
They'd lit the fire of Beltan E'en,
And danced around, and piled it high
With peat and heather and pine-tops dry.

VII.

A piper play'd a lightsome reel,
And timed the dance with toe and heel ;
While wives look'd on, as lad and lass
Trod it merrily o'er the grass.

VIII.

And Jessie (fickle and fair was she)
Sat with Evan beneath a tree,
And smiled with mingled love and pride,
And half agreed to be his bride.

IX.

The Kelpie gallop'd o'er the green—
He seemed a knight of noble mien,
And old and young stood up to see,
And wonder'd who the knight could be.

X.

His flowing locks were auburn bright,
His cheeks were ruddy, his eyes flash'd light;
And as he sprang from his good gray steed,
He look'd a gallant youth indeed.

XI.

And Jessie's fickle heart beat high,
As she caught the stranger's glancing eye :
And when he smiled, " Ah well," thought she,
" I wish this knight came courting me ! "

XII.

He took two steps towards her seat—
" Wilt thou be mine, O maiden sweet ? "
He took her lily-white hand, and sigh'd,
" Maiden, maiden, be my bride ! "

XIII.

And Jessie blush'd, and whisper'd soft—
" Meet me to-night when the moon's aloft ;
I've dream'd, fair knight, long time of thee—
I thought thou camest courting me."

XIV.

When the moon her yellow horn display'd,
Alone to the trysting went the maid ;
When all the stars were shining bright,
Alone to the trysting went the knight.

XV.

" I have loved thee long, I have loved thee well,
Maiden, oh more than words can tell !
Maiden, thine eyes like diamonds shine ;
Maiden, maiden, be thou mine ! "

XVI.

" Fair sir, thy suit I'll ne'er deny—
Though poor my lot, my hopes are high ;
I scorn a lover of low degree—
None but a knight shall marry me."

XVII.

He took her by the hand so white,
And gave her a ring of the gold so bright ;
" Maiden, whose eyes like diamonds shine—
Maiden, maiden, now thou'rt mine ! "

XVIII.

He lifted her on his steed of gray,
And they rode till morning away, away—
Over the mountain and over the moor,
And over the rocks, to the dark sea-shore.

XIX.

"We have ridden east, we have ridden west—
I'm weary, fair knight, and I fain would rest,
Say, is thy dwelling beyond the sea?
Hast thou a good ship waiting for me?"

XX.

"I have no dwelling beyond the sea,
I have no good ship waiting for thee;
Thou shalt sleep with me on a couch of foam,
And the depths of the ocean shall be thy home."

XXI.

The gray steed plunged in the billows clear,
And the maiden's shrieks were sad to hear.
"Maiden, whose eyes like diamonds shine—
Maiden, maiden, now thou'rt mine!"

XXII.

Loud the cold sea-blast did blow,
As they sank 'mid the angry waves below—
Down to the rocks where the serpents creep,
Twice five hundred fathoms deep.

XXIII.

At morn a fisherman, sailing by,
Saw her pale corse floating high;
He knew the maid by her yellow hair
And her lily skin so soft and fair.

XXIV.

Under a rock on Scarba's shore,
Where the wild winds sigh and the breakers roar,
They dug her a grave by the water clear,
Among the sea-weed salt and sere.

XXV.

And every year at Beltan E'en,
The Kelpie gallops across the green,
On a steed as fleet as the wintry wind,
With Jessie's mournful ghost behind.

XXVI.

I warn you, maids, whoever you be,
Beware of pride and vanity ;
And ere on change of love you reckon,
Beware the Kelpie of Corrievreckan.

CHARLES MACKAY.

THE ELF OF THE WOODLANDS.

A CHILD'S STORY.

IN his bed the summer sun is sleeping,
  And the air is murky and cool ;
The vapours o'er the grass are creeping,
  Or hanging above the pool ;
    But a timid gleam,
    Like a half-awake dream,
  Comes peering and peeping soon ;

Till dew-drops trickle gay
    In the spider's web to play,
And swing in his spangled festoon.
A soft beam tips the trunks and leaves
    Of this green silent wood,
And presently a net-work weaves,
    And presently a hood ;
A net-work and a hood of gold,
Spread in many a lovely fold,
    And many a gleaming band,
Silently as minutes, told
    Into a Lover's hand.

Oh, it is a silent wood
    In this early summer morning !
Even the birds are not half awake,
But whisper their chirrups in the brake,
    Like a prelude of sweet warning.
It is as if the placid hours
Hung their heads like folded flowers,
    Or like sweet flowers in bud,
Still and happy, smiling and good,
    As children in a morning dream,
Who move not—yet awake they seem,
Their close lids gilded by the beam.

There is a pretty cottage white,
    Which also seems asleep,
Dreaming in the early light—
    Its very roof and windows sleep !
Each gentle shade that fades away,
    Before the rays that following creep,
Is nothing more than dreaming play—
    The cottage surely *is* asleep !

What buzzing tickles yon oak-tree's foot,
  Bustling and busy, with nought to be seen !
There's something fidgeting at the root,
With a foo-fooing sound like a school-boy's flute,
  And a rattling like pods of dry bean !
See ! see ! there's a thing scarce five inches high,
With a comical motion and funny bright eye,
  And a look both roguish and bold—
His limbs are all antics—he skips like a flea—
His body is brown as the bark of a tree,
  Mix'd with green streaks and tarnish'd gold !

    With little legs straddling,
      He dances about—
    Pretends to be waddling—
      Then leaps with a flout
At something he sees in the bright quiet air,
And in front of the cottage he makes antics rare !
    He dances, he prances,
    Gives hiccups and kick-ups,
But all without noise is his merriment made ;
    He laughs at the little cot !
    Threatens the chimney-pot !
But soft as a moth, or as light plays with shade.

    Now he stops—
    Now he hops—
Now cautiously trips !
    On tip-toe,
    And slip-toe
He skuttles and skips ;
    Along the grass gliding,
    Half-dancing—half-sliding—
    Oft stooping—half hiding—

Then bolt upright walks,
And whispering talks
        To himself,
        Pretty elf;
And quaint sounds he utters,
Till close to the shutters
Of the cot that's still sleeping,
He climbs up close, peeping,
And pokes in each crevice his sharp little nose;
Till one shutter creaks,
And opening squeaks,
And the elfin springs down, and dances and crows!
        Till softly again,
        He climbs to the lattice,
        Taps once, twice, and thrice!
        Puffs and blows—
        And through the crack'd pane
        In he goes!

Within this cottage lived a child—
    "Toody" her name—she was not very big
You might judge by the plants and shrubs that grew
        wild,
    And o'er her head nodded or lifted a sprig.
Within the same cot there also resided
Her cousins—in love they were never divided—
    Kitty and Crocus, Tiny and Twig.
But accurate words in good time to employ,
We say "Tiny's" a small dog, and not a small boy;
And likewise explain that Grandmama Grey,
    In spectacles, tucker, and flower'd chintz gown,
Took care of them all—often grave, seldom gay,
    Yet she always half smiled when trying to frown.

Five o'clock in the morning!
    "What noise do I hear below?"

Cried Grandmama Grey. "Although it's broad day,
There's no one up, I know."
Then her head's complete adorning —
Her turret cover'd with snow,
Skull-cap and bandage, and double-frill'd night-cap,
With puff-crown and ribbon, bows, broad-strings,
and all,
Not stopping to think, and not caring what might hap,
She cast off, and threw at the opposite wall !
Crying loudly, "Come, children ! jump up with me—
There's a rat in the dairy ! run quickly and see !
Down with me, each one, as blithe as a grig—
Toody and Kitty, and Crocus and Twig !"
At once down the stairs they ran scrambling and
fumbling,
In night-gowns and night-caps—all laughing and
jumbling,
With Tiny between their legs, barking and tumbling.

Down at last they are safely landed,
Dusky the parlour—the shutters closed,
Though one swings a-jar (which the Elfin's hand did),
By green blinds the light is still opposed.
So one by one, some rosy, some pale—
As Indians cautiously pass through a mead,
Holding each other by night-gown tail,
Dame Grey and the children in silence proceed.

They reach the dairy—pause at the door ;
They look at each other, then clap their hands,
And in they bounce, as a wave on the shore
Scatters its foam on the lonely sands,
On all sides they spread, and stare round about,
But soon they huddle together in fear,
For behind a milk-jug, under the spout,
They see a small figure that's wondrous queer !

449

It is golden, and greenish, and earthy brown,
    With a perking nose and a pointed chin,
It has very bright eyes and a funny frown,
    With a russetin, apple's network skin.
They see him ! they see him !
    He knows it, too well !—
        They flee him ! they flee him !—
    In terror pell-mell !
But Tiny springs up—and around a milk-pan [can !—
Gives chase !—now they scour round as fast as they

They whirl round so swift their two bodies seem one,
And like a dark band on a humming-top spun.
Dame Grey and the children ran back from their nook,—
The chase takes away their breath as they look !
Till at length with a noise like a bark, laugh, and scream,
The elf leapt in !—and swam across three pans of cream !
            On the opposite side,
            He had quickly espied
            In the wall a small shelf,
            And there landed himself.
            " We've lost him ! we've lost him ! "
            The children all cried !
        But Grandmama Grey,
        I am happy to say,
        Being in her own dairy,
        Was wise as a fairy,
            And quick with a jelly-bag,
            At the shelf's end,
            Into its belly-swag
                Swept our small friend !

Now you must know that good Dame Grey
    Had prudence at her fingers' ends,
And to the parlour leads the way,
    But no one knows what she intends.

Said she, "Now, all go up and dress,
  I'll leave the bag upon the floor
Mouth downwards ; Tiny's watchfulness
  Shall guard the window, chimney, door."
So Tiny came, and gravely stood
  With both ears cock'd, and nose down bent,
While with as fix'd an attitude
  The pointed bag stood, like a tent !

Soon they were dress'd, and down they came ;
  Breakfast was ready, the tea-kettle singing ;
Toast, hot rolls, water-cresses, and ham,—
  And the parlour-bell still for more egg-cups ringing !
But mute as a tree, with a truant notching it !
Stood the jelly-bag tent, with Tiny watching it.

Up rose little Toody, and said, "Don't you think
  An Elf of the woods would like something to drink ?
Coffee or tea, by way of exhorter
  Not to turn sulky—perhaps, milk-and-water !"
So under one edge of the jelly-bag tent
  Toody a saucer cautiously push'd,
Then roll'd an egg under with merriment,
  Though silently all in the room sat hush'd.
Ten minutes they listened—and then—shall I tell ?
They all plainly heard the crack of a shell.

"Away with the tea-things !" said Grandmama Grey ;
In a twinkling the tea-things were taken away !
And Martha ran back to see what they meant
To do with the small rogue under the tent.
Cried Dame Grey, "Bring the bird-cage—look sharp—
  and run quicker !"
It once was a blackbird's, and made of white wicker.

The bird-cage was brought, and Grandmama Grey
Took the jelly-bag up in her carefullest way,
Clapt its mouth to the open door—shook it—at last
In popp'd the Elf!—the cage-door was made fast !
Now, what do you think the small prisoner did?
   Shed many tears, and jibber'd, and groan'd?
Crouch'd at the bottom, d'ye fancy he did,
   And there his sad capture and fate bemoan'd?
Nothing like this : with one spring and ten kicks
   He climbed to the perch, and himself he seated,
Like a young thing practising calisthenics,
   With his hands on his pole, as if tired and heated.

Toddy ran close to the cage—so did Crocus ;
Twig cried, " Here's mischief and hocus-pocus ! "
And Kitty stared smiling ; her soft hazel eyes
With wonder seem'd double their natural size.
But the Elf met their looks without a wince,
While his cheek was yellow and tart as quince,
And his tongue at one side thrust a bulb on the skin
As the sight of his left eye slid out and in.
He sat on his perch, not the least in despair,
But swinging his little legs—and, I declare,
With a perking, half-winking, impertinent air.

Dame Grey with her spectacles now rose up,
   " Who are you, little sir? and what may you be?
Do you know you have broken my best China cup,
   And spoilt all my cream?—now, answer to me !
Tell us your story from first to last—
   Where you were born—where educated—
Or here a captive for life you stay fast !—
   Begin, sir, at once—all must be stated."

Rough the crown of the Elf did bristle,
His brutus rose like a flowering thistle,
Till his anger through his nose did whistle;
But his feelings he master'd, and tried to look
Demure as a good child over his book.
Some yellow of egg he rubb'd off his chin,
And stuck like a buttercup on his shin,
Then shrugg'd his shoulders up in a hunch,
With a wheezing squeal, and a noise like Punch,
Though not half so loud.   And now with a sneeze,
Like a parrot's, who suffers much from a cold,
His account of his life among the trees
He thus, in his way, began to unfold.

" Nine white witches sat in a circle close,
    With their backs against a greenwood tree,
As around the dead-nettle's summer stem
    Its woolly white blossoms you see.
            Tack-a-rack, tangle tang, twangle tee !
                    Rills and hills,
                    Lawns and horns,
                    Hedges, sedges,
                    Rushes, thrushes,
                        Twangle dee !

" With hooded heads bent 'neath the broad green shade,
    And hands laid flat on each knee,
They sat, as around the death-nettle's stem
    Its beldame-shaped bloom you may see.
            Tack-a-rack, tangle tang, twangle tee !
                    Woods and broods,
                    Birds and herds,
                    Eggs and curds,
                    Osiers, rosiers,—
                        Tangle dee ɩ

" Now the witches so white they worked a charm
    For the life of my mother and me,
And said in the woodlands we ever should dwell,
    From man's knavish fingers free.
        Tangle fangle, jangle hangle, wrangle see!
            Guns and runs,
            Hops and pops,
            Nettings, frettings,
            Pools and fools—
                Dangle dee !

"Then from hedges and ditches, these old lady-witches,
    Took bird-weed and rag-weed, and spear-grass for
      me,
And they wove me a bower, 'gainst the snow-storm or
    shower,
    In a dry old hollow beech tree.
        Tangle dangle, suns and funs, twangle tee!
            Sticks and tricks,
            Light and sprites,
            Moons, festoons,
            Glooms, mushrooms,
                Tangle dee !

" My nest-home inside, is dark, warm, and soft
    As the sable-hair'd breast of a panting bee ;
And never in my life will I have an elfin wife,
    Till the prettiest comes to court me.
        Twangle tangle, kisses blisses, tangle tee !
            Courts and sports,
            Eyes and sighs,
            Peeps and leaps,
            Hands and bands,
            Huts and nuts—
                Twangle twee !

Ivy wreaths,
Flowering heaths,
Jays and fays,
Owls and fogs,
Bats and frogs,
Holes and moles,
Music sound
Under ground—
                    Twangle dee!
Twining, shining,
Dances, prances,
Berries, cherries,
Sorrels, laurels,
Reed-pipe, seed ripe,
Burrows, furrows,
Habits, rabbits,
Paths and crosses,
Plots and mosses,
Hares and stags,
Dwarfs and hags,
Shrubs all burry,
Creatures furry,
Wren and titmouse,
Wasp and woodlouse—
                    Twangle tee!
Races, graces,
Woodland faces,
Quaint grimaces,
Silver gushes,
Tall bull-rushes,
Rambles, scrambles,
Bogs and brambles,
Buzzes, fuzzes,
Trailing briers,
Red wood-fires,
Squirrels, jackdaws,

Things with black claws,
Legs, horns, eyes,
Blythe butterflies,
Rush-knot shoe-tie,
Peeps of blue sky,
Distant steeple,
Bee and beetle,
Fairy people,
Small legs fleetest,
Echoes sweetest,
Joy completest—
                    Twangle tee !
Ri-rigdum, dingle shade-laugh, tingle dee ! "

Each look'd at the other—none knew what to say.
" This won't do for me ! " said Grandmama Grey ;
" None of your hoaxing about white witches,
Nettles and nonsense, and hedges and ditches ;
I never before heard so clever a blade
At an answer in genuine rhodomontade.
Why do you prattle of woodland and stream ?
    What do I care how your small heels you kick up ?
You know you came here to steal *cake* and drink
        cream ;
    And, besides, you have broken a china tea-cup ! "

Hereat the Elf gazed up on high,
    Through the cage-top bars with rueful gloom,
And then he gave a little sigh,
    Fixing his eyes on Martha's broom ;
And meditated thoughtfully.
    But presently he cast a glance
At Toody, who was winking nigh ;
    And now this Elf with nonchalance
Look'd round and shouted pleasantly,

" I vow, by the tom-tit's foolish ways,
  By the mole's front claws and his pin-hole eye,
The woodpecker's thorn-tongue and groundless
          dismays,
  I have told my biography faithfully."
Again at Toody a look he stole,
Then coolly resumed his rigmarole.

" Loitering once in a wood," he said,
Cocking his nose with a side-bent head,—
" A wood full of rabbit-runs, spaces, and turns,
And crowded regiments of feathery ferns,
With all sorts of groundlings pleasant to see,
Such as cup-moss and wild anemone,—
I sat me down in a silent nook,
  By a rill that pearl'd from a grassy dell,
And being in want of an excellent book,
  I took up a pebble, which did as well.
I pondered much on its class and merit ;
Its natural secrets my heart did ferret,—
I consider'd it in a learned spirit ;
  And while I was thus at study,
I heard near at hand a fussing and spirting,
And a ruffling sound of dipping and flirting,
  'Neath a morning sky all ruddy.

On tiptoe I trip—o'er the bushes I look—
And close at the red-gravell'd edge of the brook,
  There stood a robin bathing !
He ruffled his feathers with a spattering sound,
And made himself look like a fussy round,
  Or some fairy's curious plaything,
With a spangly shower all flying and splashing,
In a circle of water-drops showering and flashing !
          But presently—
          His eye—his eye !——"

" His eye—his eye ! " all the children cried—
" What of his eye ? "   The Elf, aside,
Once more at Toody stole a glance,
And Toody a quiet nod gave askance,
As much as to say, " I'll find you a chance."
And then the Elf gave a downward squint
At the close cage-door, by way of a hint ;
And, after scratching his apricot cheek,
Of the robin again he proceeded to speak,—
Jumping down to the floor of the cage,
And acting a " robin " as if on the stage.

"His eye ! his eye !
The clear round mirror of jet and light,
        Caught a glimpse of me.
He bobbed—took wing—and was out of sight.
        Well, good folks—well !
        I have more to tell !
Then I stood up in the rabbit-path,
   Winding along the low banks of the rill,
Where I saw the robin taking his bath,
   And I fancy I see him still !

True, as I say, he came back once more,
   With a fluster'd air, and in anger ; I vow
He look'd like an alderman lecturing the poor,
But meaning at last to—*unlock the cage-door !*
        Methinks, I see him now !
   Along and across, he hops and he flits
        Just so !—on my word—just so !
   Then suddenly—look, there he sits
        Upon a topmost twig !
   He took a flight—and then a hop—
        Again a flight,
        Then perch'd so light
   Upon the twig's tip-top !

Look at his large bright eye,
  Very round and very black ;
    Now he bobs, and now he bows,
      Incessantly,
  With head, and tail, and back ;
    Eob, tail—and now bob, nose,
      Up and down he goes,
  Then off he flies in a crack !
Upon a tall tree bough,
There—there ! I see him now !
    Come, Bob, come !
    He sits quite dumb—
    What cares he for a crumb—
Look at his breast so red !
Again he bows his head,
Bobs and bows—ruffles his wings—
Now smoothes them down, and then he sings.
How he sings and warbles sweet !
    No more bobbing,
    Hob-and-nobbing,
Quiet he sits, and fills the air
With music delicate and rare ;
And now he glances at his feet,
Then like a gentleman complete
  He bobs again—gives one quick bow,
    As I do now !—
Points down his tail, and up his nose—
    And *off* he goes !"

"Run, Tiny—run !—Oh, Kitty, Twig, and Crocus !
The little wretch is gone !—oh, villain, thus to joke us!
Run, Toody—run !—you, you are the deceiver
That loosen'd the cage-door !—I'm surely in a fever !
Tiny, chase him—Tiny, catch him !
    Oh, Kitty, Twig, and Crocus—
The robin redbreast story was only meant to hoax us !

Away—away—away !
　Come all into the wood !
Follow me, I say, I say, I say,
　Through brambles, weeds, and mud !"
Oh, none shall run to-day
So fast as Granny Grey,
　She hath the youngest blood !

Off they all ran trooping,
And hallooing and hooping,
Beneath the low boughs stooping,
　　Right through the wood,
For Grandmama Grey,
Like an old duck, led the way,
When a string of ducks trudge to a flood.
　　Then came Kitty, side by side
　　With Toody, who oft cried,
" Oh, Kitty dear, was ever such rare fun, fun, fun !"
　　And Crocus close to Twig,
　　Both scampered in a jig,
For they knew the Elf his freedom-race had won, won,
　won.

　　As for him, the roguish Elf,
　　He took good care of himself ;
His mites of legs they twinkled as he fled, fled, fled !
　　He was scarcely seen, indeed,
　　He so glistened with his speed,
And his hair streamed out like silver grass behind his
　head !

　　Now leaping here, now there,
　　Tiny barking everywhere,
Through undergrowth and thicket made his way with
　nose and claw,

Till suddenly the party
Met, full drive, with laughter hearty,
Florry, Pay, Bow, Carry, Minnie, Ganner, Andy, Ock,
and Daw !

Such a meeting—such quick greeting—
Such explaining and repeating !
All confusion, no one listening, but all for the chase ;
So off the party pack
To follow the Elf's track,
And Granny Grey was foremost still in this mad race !

Now flew buttons, laces, bands,
While with burning face and hands,
Through and through, and up and down, they troop with
shout and crow !
Under, over, and across
Shrubs, tangles, trunks, and moss,
Till their hearts are almost bursting, and they gasp, and
puff, and blow !
They struggle and they strive,
Droop—lag—and then revive ;
And once again they speed along and wish for wings to
fly ;
They grow deaf and dizzy-eyed—
With pains in head and side ;
But the Elf they cannot overtake—'tis all in vain to try !

So the party wild with heat,
And defeat—so complete—
To the cottage stagger and retreat—
Oh, oh, oh !
And, with fagg'd and streaming faces, they all sit down
on the floor,
Their clothes green from bark of trees—
Torn and mudded to the knees—

With faces like red-lion signs, and feet all sore !
 There they sit, a good long hour,
  As for moving !—they have no such power ;
And Martha with hot water comes, each hand and face
 to wash.
  And then, still lounging on the ground,
  Cups of tea are handed round,
Their dinners they had lost, while they hunted brake and
 bush.

  All hungry as young hawks,
  How the toast and butter " walks,"
With legs of fowl down hunters' throats, who seem'd just
 now half dead ;
  But soon they laugh and shout,
  Eat and drink, and loll about.
Till at last with laughing kisses they all troop off to bed.

  But where to sleep none knew,
   For the cottage was but small,
  Yet by Dame Grey's arrangement
   There was room enough for all.
  Three slept upon the floor
   Of the largest room upstairs,
  And in the parlour, four,
   On sofa, rug, and chairs.
  The night was warm and pleasant—
   One filled the window seat ;
  And two slept in the summer-house—
   And, oh, it was so sweet !

  Within a very little nook
   Toody always slept alone ;
  Its strip of window stole a look
   Over the lawn and hay-rick cone.

Within the open lattice crept
　　Some jasmine from the cottage wall,
And to the breathing of her sleep,
　　Softly swayed, with rise and fall.
But something else comes creeping in,
　　As softly from the starry night,—
The Elf !—'tis he !—first peeping in,
　　Now like a moth doth he alight !
He trips up to the little bed,
　　And near it hangs a full-blown rose,
Then in the middle of the flower
　　Places a light that gleams and glows.
It is a glow-worm from the lea,
　　And lighting up the rose's heart,
A fairy grot it seems to be—
　　Where dream-thoughts live and ne'er depart.
And now the Elf once more is gone
　　Into the woodlands wild,
Leaving his blessing thus to shine
　　Upon the dreaming child.

R. H. HORNE.

TWO FAIRIES IN A GARDEN.

1.　" Whither goest, brother Elf? "

2.　" The sun is weak—to warm myself
　　In a thick red tulip's core.
　　Whither thou ?"

1.　　　　　　" Till day be o'er,
　　To the dim and deep snow-palace
　　Of the closest lily-chalice,

Where is veil'd the light of noon
To be like my Lady's moon.
Thou art of the day, I ween?"

2. "Yet I not disown our Queen,
Nor at Lysc' am backward found,
When the mighty Feast comes round;
When She spreads abroad her power
To proclaim a midnight hour
For the pale blue Fays like thee
And the ruddy Elves like me
To mingle in a charmèd ring
With a perfect welcoming;
Guarded from the moon-stroke cold,
And wisp that scares us on the wold,"

1. "Swift that Night is drawing near,
When your abrupt and jovial cheer,
Mixes in our misty dance,
Meeting else by rarest chance.
We love dark undew'd recesses
Of the leafy wildernesses,
Or to hide in some cold flow'r,
Shelter'd from the sunlight hour,
And more afflictive mortal eye."

2. "Gladly, gladly, do I spy
Human children playing nigh,
Feel, and so must you, the grace
Of a loving human face.
Else why come you in this place?
O, my Sister, if we might
Show ourselves to mortal sight
Far more often! if they knew
Half the friendly turns we do!

Even now, a gentle thought
Would pay my service dimly wrought,
Round these winding garden-walks,
Fruits and flow'rs and leaves and stalks.
Paler favourites of the noon,
Can ye give or take such boon ? "

1. "Chantings, Brother, hear you might,
Softly sung through still of night ;
Calling from the wëird North
Dreams like distant echoes forth,
Till through curtain'd shades they creep,
To inlay the gloomy floor of sleep
For babes, and souls that babe-like are :
So we bless them from afar
Like a faint but favouring star.
—But tell me how in fields or bowers
Thou hast spent these morning hours ? "

2. " Through the tall hedge I have been,
Shadowy wall of crusted green,
Within whose heart the birds are seen.
Speeding swiftly thence away
To the crowning chestnut-spray,
I watch'd a Tyrant steal along
Would slay the sweet Thrush in her song ;
Warned, she soon broke off from singing,
There we left the branchlet swinging.
Whispering Robin, down the walk,
News of poising, pouncing Hawk,
The Sycamore I next must strew
On every leaf with honey-dew.
And hither now from clouds I run,
For all my morning work is done."

1. " Alas, I wither in the sun,
   Witless drawn to leave my nest
   Ere the day be laid to rest !
   But to-night we lightly troop
   By the young Moon's silver hoop ;
   Weaving wide our later ranks
   As on evening river-banks
   Shifting crowds of midges glance
   Through mazes of their airy dance :
   O might you come, O might you see
   All our shadow'd revelry !
   Yet the next night shall be rarer,
   Next and next and next, still fairer ;
   We are waxing every night,
   Till our joy be full and bright ;
   Then as slowly do we wane
   With gentle loss that makes no pain.
   For thus are we with life endued :
   Ye, I trow, have rougher food."

2. " Yes : with fragrant soul we're fed
   Of every flower whose cheek is red,
   Shunning yellow, blue, and white ;
   And southward go, at the nightingale's flight.
   Many the Faery Nations be.
   Oh ! how I long, I long to see
   The moonèd midnight of our Feast,
   Flushing amber through the east,
   When every cap in Elfindom
   Into that great ring shall come,
   Owf and Elf and Fairy blended,
   Till th' imperial time be ended !
   Even those fantastic Sprites
   Lay aside their dear delights
   Of freakish mischief and annoyance
   In the universal joyance,

One of whom I saw of late
As I peep'd through window-grate,
(Under roof I may not enter)
Haunt the housewife to torment her,
Tangle up her skeins of silk,
Throw a mouse into her milk,
Hide her thimble, scorch her roast,
Quickly drive her mad almost;
And I too vex'd, because I would
Have brought her succour if I could.
—But where shall this be holden, say?
Far away?"

1.   "O, far away,
Over river must we fly,
Over the sea, and the mountain high,
Over city, seen afar
Like a low and misty star,—
Soon beneath us glittering
Like million spark-worms.   But our wing,
For the flight will ne'er suffice.
Some are training Flittermice,
I a Silver Moth."

2.   "Be ware
How I'll thrid the vaulted air!
A Dragon-fly with glassy wings,
Born beside the meadow-springs,
That can arrow-swiftly glide
Thorough the glowing eventide,
Nor at twilight-fall grow slack,
Shall bear me on his long blue back.
Dew-stars, meteors of the night,
May not strike him with affright,
He can needle through the wood,
That's like a green earth-chainèd cloud,
Mountain-summits deftly rake,
Draw swift line o'er plain and lake.

If at Lysco I be last,
Other elves must journey fast.
Lu a vo ! "

1.   " But, Elf, I rede,
Of all your Herbs take special heed.
Our Mistress tholes no garden flowers,
Though we have freedom of these bowers.
Tell me what you mean to treasure,
Each in 's atom ? "

2.   " Gold-of-Pleasure,
Medic, Plumeseed, Fountain-arrow,
Vervain, Hungry-grass, and Yarrow,
Quatrefoil and Melilot. "

1. " These are well.   And I have got
Moonwort and the Filmy Fern,
Gather'd nicely on the turn.
Wo to Fairy that shall bring
Bugloss for an offering,
Toad-flax, Barley of the Wall,
Enchanter's Nightshade, worst of all.
—Oh, brother, hush ! I faint with fear !
A mortal footstep threatens near. "

2. " None can see us, none can hear.
Yet, to make thee less afraid,
Hush we both as thou hast pray'd.
I will seek the verse to spell
Written round my dark flow'r's bell,
To sing at sunset.   So, Farewell ! "

WILLIAM ALLINGHAM.

✳

ELFIN SONG.

I.

FAR in the western ocean's breast
The summer fairies have found a nest ;
The heavens ever unclouded smile
Over the breadth of their beautiful isle ;
Through it a hundred streamlets flow,
In spangled paths, to the sea below,
And woo the vales that beside them lie
With a low and tremulous minstrelsy.
The elfin brood have homes they love
In the earth below and skies above ;
But the haunt which of all they love the best
Is the palm-crowned isle, in the ocean's breast,
⠀⠀⠀That mortals call Canary ;
And many an Ariel, blithesome, airy,
And each laughing fay and lithesome fairy,
Know well the mystical way in the West
⠀⠀⠀To the sweet isle of Canary.

II.

With an ever-sounding choral chant,
And a clear, cerulean, wild desire
To clasp that fairy island nigher,
The sinuous waves of ocean pant ;
For here all natural things are free
To mingle in passionate harmony.
The light from their mirror turns away
With a golden splendour, in the day,
But nightly, when coroneted Even
Marshals the shining queen of heaven,
There gleams a silvery scenery,
From the rim of the great prismatic sea
⠀⠀⠀Around the isle of Canary

To the central crags of Pisgatiri,
Where the crested eagle builds his eyry,
    Scanning the shores of sweet Canary.

III.

Lustrously sailing here and there,
Afloat in the beatific air,
Birds, of purple and blue and gold,
Pour out their music manifold ;
All day long in the leas they sing,
While the sun-kissed flowers are blossoming ;
At eve, when the dew-drop feeds the rose,
And the fragrant water-lilies close,
The marvellous-throated nightingale
With a dying music floods each vale,
Till the seaward breezes, listening, stay
To catch the harmony of his lay
    And cool the air of Canary ;
And thus the melodies ever vary,
In the vales of the ocean aviary,
    In the blissful valleys of sweet Canary.

IV.

The Elle-King's palace was builded there
By elves of water and earth and air ;
Lovingly worked each loyal sprite,
And it grew to life in a summer night.
Over the sheen of its limpid moat,
Wafted along, in a magic boat,
By fairy wings that fan the sails,
And eddying through enchanted vales,
Through walls of amber and crystal gates,
We come where a fairy warder waits ;
And so, by many a winding way
Where sweet bells jingle and fountains play,

To the inmost, royalest room of all,—
The elfin monarch's reception-hall,
    The pearl and pride of Canary !
To guard its fastness the elves are wary,
And no weird thing, of pleasure chary,
    Can enter with evil in sweet Canary !

V.

All that saddens, and care and pain,
Are banished far from that fair domain ;
There forever, by day and night,
Is naught but pleasance and love's delight ;
Daily, the Genii of the flowers
Shade with beauty a hundred bowers ;
Nightly, the Gnomes of precious stones
Emblazon and light a hundred thrones ;
And the Elves of the field, so swift and mute,
Bring wine and honey and luscious fruit ;
And the Sylphs of the air, at noontide, cool
The depths of each bower and vestibule ;
And all are gay,—from the tricksome Fay
Who flutters in woodlands far away,
To the best-beloved attendant Elf,
And the royal heart of the king himself,
    Who rules in bright Canary ;
And the labouring Fairies are blithe and merry,
Who press the juice from the swollen berry
    That reddens the vines of sweet Canary.

VI.

What if there be a fated day
When the Faëry Isle shall pass away,
And its beautiful groves and fountains seem
The myths of a long, delicious dream !

A century's joys shall first repay
Our hearts, for the evil of that day ;
And the Elfin-King has sworn to wed
A daughter of Earth, whose child shall be,
By cross and water hallowéd,
From the fairies' doom forever free.
What if there be a fated day !
It is far away ! it is far away !
Maiden, fair Maiden, I, who sing
Of this summer isle, am the island king.
I come from its joys to make thee mine :
Half of my kingdom shall be thine ;
Our horses of air and ocean wait—
Then hasten, and share the Elle-King's state
      In the sweet isle of Canary ;
And many an Ariel, blithsome, airy,
And each laughing fay and lithesome fairy,
Shall rovingly hover around and over thee,
And the love of a king shall evermore cover thee,
      Nightly and daily in sweet Canary.

EDMUND CLARENCE STEDMAN.

THE FERLIE.

A FERLIE came ben to me yestreen,
A lady jimp an' sma',
Wi' a milk-white snood an' a kirtle green,
Yellow an' roun were her bonny e'en,
And she said, " Will ye come awa'?

" Will ye gang wi' me to the Elflyn Knowe,
To milk our queene's coo ? "

"Na, na," quo' I, "I maun shear my sheep,
I've my barn to bigg, an' my corn to reap,
Sae I canna come the noo."

The ferlie skirled as she turned to gae,
For an angry elf was she,
"O a wilfu' man maun hae his way,
An I mak' sma' doot but ye'll rue the day
That ye wouldna gang wi' me."

"O, ance again will ye speir at me
An' I'll aiblins come awa'?"
"O I'll come again to your yetts," quo' she,
"When broom blooms bright on yon rowan-tree
An' the laverock sings i' th' snaw!"

GRAHAM R. TOMSON.

Miscellaneous.

THE FOUNTAIN OF THE FAIRIES.

THERE is a fountain in the forest call'd
The Fountain of the Fairies : when a child
With a delightful wonder I have heard
Tales of the elfin tribe who on its banks
Hold midnight revelry.   An ancient oak,
The goodliest of the forest, grows beside ;
Alone it stands, upon a green grass plat,
By the woods bounded like some little isle.
It ever hath been deem'd their favourite tree,
They love to lie and rock upon its leaves,
And bask in moonshine.   Here the woodman leads
His boy, and showing him the green-sward mark'd
With darker circlets, says the midnight dance
Hath traced the rings, and bids him spare the tree.
Fancy had cast a spell upon the place
Which made it holy; and the villagers
Would say that never evil thing approach'd
Unpunish'd there.   The strange and fearful pleasure
Which fill'd me by that solitary spring,
Ceased not in riper years ; and now it wakes
Deeper delight, and more mysterious awe.

ROBERT SOUTHEY.

SONGS OF THE PIXIES.

[The Pixies, in the superstitions of Devonshire, are a race of beings invisibly small, and harmless or friendly to man. At a small distance from a village in that county, half-way up a wood-covered hill, is an excavation, called the Pixies' parlour. The roots of old trees form its ceiling; and on its sides are innumerable ciphers, among which the author discovered his own cipher and those of his brothers, cut by the hand of their childhood. At the foot of the hill flows the river Otter. To this place the author conducted a party of young ladies, during the summer months of the year 1793; one of whom, of stature elegantly small, and of complexion colourless yet clear, was proclaimed the Fairy Queen: on which occasion, and at which time, the following irregular ode was written.]

I.

WHOM the untaught shepherds call
    PIXIES in their madrigal,
Fancy's children, here we dwell :
    Welcome, ladies ! to our cell.
Here the wren of softest note
    Builds its nest and warbles well ;
Here the blackbird strains his throat ;
    Welcome, ladies ! to our cell.

II.

When fades the moon all shadowy-pale,
And scuds the cloud before the gale,
Ere morn with living gems bedight
Streaks the East with purple light,
We sip the furze flowers fragrant dews,
Clad in robes of rainbow hues
Richer than the deepened bloom
That glows on summer's scented plume :

Or sport amid the rosy gleam,
Soothed by the distant-tinkling team,
While lusty labour, scouting sorrow,
Bids the dame a glad good-morrow,
Who jogs th' accustomed road along,
And paces cheery to her cheering song.

III.

But not our filmy pinion
We scorch amid the blaze of day
When noon-tide's fiery-tressed minion
    Flashes the fervid ray.
    Aye from the sultry heat
    We to the cave retreat,
O'ercanopied by huge roots intertwined
With wildest texture, blackened o'er with age ;
Round them their mantles green the ivies bind,
    Beneath whose foliage pale,
    Fanned by the unfrequent gale,
We shield us from the tyrant's mid-day rage.

IV.

Thither while the murmuring throng
Of wild-bees hum their drowsy song,
By indolence and fancy brought,
A youthful bard, " unknown to fame,"
Woos the queen of solemn thought,
And heaves the gentle mis'ry of a sigh,
    Gazing with tearful eye,
As round our sandy grot appear
Many a rudely sculptured name
    To pensive mem'ry dear !

Weaving gay dreams of sunny-tinctured hue
    We glance before his view :
O'er his hushed soul our soothing witch'ries shed,
And twine our faery garlands round his head.

V.

    When evening's dusky car
    Crowned with her dewy star
Steals o'er the fading sky in shadowy flight ;
    On leaves of aspen trees
    We tremble to the breeze,
Veiled from the grosser ken of mortal sight.
    Or, haply at the visionary hour,
Along our wild sequestered walk,
We listen to th' enamoured rustic's talk ;
Heave with the heavings of the maiden's breast,
Where young-eyed loves have built their turtle nest ;
    Or guide of soul-subduing power
Th' electric flash, that from the melting eye
Darts the fond question and the soft reply.

VI.

Or thro' the mystic ringlets of the vale
We flash our faery feet in gamesome prank ;
Or, silent-sandalled, pay our defter court
Circling the spirit of the western gale,
Where, wearied with his flower-caressing sport,
Supine he slumbers on a violet bank !
Then with quaint music hymn the parting gleam,
By lonely Otter's sleep-persuading stream ;
Or where his wave with loud unquiet song
Dashed o'er the rocky channel froths along ;
Or where, his silver waters smoothed to rest,
The tall tree's shadow sleeps upon his breast.

VII.

Hence ! thou lingerer, light !
Eve saddens into night.
Mother of wildly-working dreams ! we view
The sombre hours, that round thee stand
With down-cast eyes (a duteous band !),
Their dark robes dripping with the heavy dew.
Sorceress of the ebon throne !
Thy power the Pixies own,
When round thy raven brow
Heaven's lucent roses glow,
And clouds, in wat'ry colours drest,
Float in light drapery o'er thy sable vest ;
What time the pale moon sheds a softer ray,
Mellowing the woods beneath its pensive beam :
For 'mid the quiv'ring light 'tis ours to play,
Aye dancing to the cadence of the stream.

VIII.

Welcome, ladies ! to the cell,
Where the blameless Pixies dwell,
But thou, sweet nymph ! proclaimed our faery queen,
With what obeisance meet
Thy presence shall we greet ?
For lo ! attendant on thy steps are seen
Graceful ease in artless stole,
And white-robed purity of soul,
With honour's softer mien :
Mirth of the loosely-flowing hair
And meek-eyed pity eloquently fair,
Whose tearful cheeks are lovely to the view,
As snow-drop wet with dew.

IX.

Unboastful Maid ! tho' now the lily pale
  Transparent grace thy beauties meek ;
Yet ere again along the impurpling vale,
The purpling vale and elfin-haunted grove,
Young Zephyr his fresh flowers profusely throws,
  We'll tinge with livelier hues thy cheek !
And haply from the nectar-breathing rose
  Extract a blush of love !

SAMUEL TAYLOR COLERIDGE.

FAIRY FAVOURS.

WOULD'ST thou wear the gift of immortal bloom ?
Would'st thou smile in scorn at the shadowy tomb ?
Drink of this cup ! it is richly fraught
With balm from the gardens of genii brought ;
Drink, and the spoiler shall pass thee by,
When the young all scattered like rose-leaves lie.

And would not the youth of my soul be gone,
If the loved had left me, one by one ?
Take back the cup that may never bless,
The gift that would make me brotherless ;
How should I live with no kindred eye
To reflect mine immortality ?

Would'st thou have empire, by sign or spell,
Over the mighty in air that dwell ?
Would'st thou call the spirits of shore and steep
To fetch thee jewels from ocean's deep ?
Wave but this rod, and a viewless band,
Slaves to thy will, shall around thee stand.

And would not fear, at my coming then,
Hush every voice in the homes of men?
Would not bright eyes in my presence quail?
Young cheeks with a nameless thrill turn pale?
No gift be mine that aside would turn
The human love for whose founts I yearn!

Would'st thou then read through the hearts of those
Upon whose faith thou hast sought repose?
Wear this rich gem! it is charm'd to show
When a change comes over affection's glow,
Look on its flushing or fading hue,
And learn if the trusted be false or true!

Keep, keep the gem, that I still may trust,
Though my heart's wealth be but pour'd on dust!
Let not a doubt in my soul have place,
To dim the light of a loved one's face;
Leave to the earth its warm sunny smile—
That glory would pass could I look on guile!

Say, then, what boon of my power shall be,
Favour'd of spirits! pour'd forth on thee?
Thou scornest the treasures of wave and mine,
Thou wilt not drink of the cup divine,
Thou art fain with a mortal's lot to rest—
Answer me! how may I grace it best?

Oh! give me no sway o'er the powers unseen,
But a human heart where my own may lean!
A friend, one tender and faithful friend,
Whose thoughts' free current with mine may blend,
And leaving not either on earth alone,
Bid the bright calm close of our lives be one!

FELICIA HEMANS.

WATER-LILIES.

A FAIRY SONG.

COME away, elves ! while the dew is sweet,
Come to the dingles where fairies meet ;
Know that the lilies have spread their bells
O'er all the pools in our forest dells ;
Stilly and lightly their vases rest
On the quivering sleep of the water's breast,
Catching the sunshine through leaves that throw
To their scented bosoms an emerald glow ;
And a star from the depth of each pearly cup,
A golden star unto heaven looks up,
As if seeking its kindred where bright they lie,
Set in the blue of the summer sky.
—Come away ! under arching boughs we'll float,
Making those urns each a fairy boat ;
We'll row them with reeds o'er the fountains free,
And a tall flag-leaf shall our streamer be,
And we'll send out wild music so sweet and low,
It shall seem from the bright flower's heart to flow,
As if 'twere a breeze with a flute's low sigh,
Or water drops train'd into melody.
—Come away ! for the midsummer sun grows strong,
And the life of the lily may not be long.

FELICIA HEMANS.

FANTASIES.

I.

I'M weary, I'm weary,—this cold world of ours;
I will go dwell afar, with fairies and flowers.
Farewell to the festal, the hall of the dance,
Where each step is a study, a falsehood each glance ;
Where the vain are displaying, the vapid are yawning ;
Where the beauty of night, the glory of dawning,
Are wasted, as Fashion, that tyrant, at will
Makes war on sweet nature, and exiles her still.

II.

I'm weary, I'm weary,—I'm off with the wind :
Can I find a worse fate than the one left behind ?
—Fair beings of moonlight, gay dwellers in air,
O show me your kingdom ! O let me dwell there !
I see them, I see them !—how sweet it must be
To sleep in yon lily !—is there room in't for me ?
I have flung my clay fetters ; and now I but wear
A shadowy seeming, a likeness of air.

III.

Go harness my chariot, the leaf of an oak ;
A butterfly stud, and a tendril my yoke.
Go swing me a hammock, the poles mignionette ;
I'll rock with its scent in the gossamer net.
Go fetch me a courser : yon reed is but slight,
Yet far is the distance 'twill bear me to-night.
I must have a throne,—ay, yon mushroom may stay,
It has sprung in a night, 'twill be gather'd next day :
And fit is such throne for my brief fairy reign ;
For alas ! I'm but dreaming, and dreams are but vain.

L. E. L.

THE CITY OF GOLD.

YEARS onward have swept,
  Aye, long ages have rolled—
Since the billows first slept
  O'er the City of Gold !

'Neath its eddy of white
  Where the green wave is swelling,
In their halls of delight
  Are the fairy tribes dwelling.

And but seldom the eye
  Of a mortal may scan,
Where those palaces high
  Rise unaided by man.

Yet, at times the waves sever,
  And then you may view
The yellow walls ever
  'Neath the ocean's deep blue.

But I warn thee, O man !
  Never seek to behold,
Where the crystal streams ran
  In the City of Gold !

Like a beauty with guile,
  When some young knight has found her,
There is death in her smile,
  And dark ruin around her !

Like a poet's first dream
  In his longings for glory;
A dagger whose gleam
  With the life-blood is gory.

Like wishes possessed,
   And for which we have panted,
When we find us unblest,
   Tho' our prayers have been granted.

Like ought that's forbidden
   Weak man to behold,
Death and sorrow are hid in
   The City of Gold.

Rash youth ! dost thou view it,
   The ransom thou'lt pay,
Alas ! thou must rue it,
   Death takes thee to-day !

ANONYMOUS.

THE FAIRIES.

Up the airy mountain,
   Down the rushy glen,
We daren't go a-hunting
   For fear of little men;
Wee folk, good folk,
   Trooping all together ;
Green jacket, red cap,
   And white owl's feather !

Down along the rocky shore
   Some make their home,
They live on crispy pancakes
   Of yellow tide-foam ;

Some in the reeds
   Of the black mountain lake,
With frogs for their watch-dogs,
   All night awake.

High on the hill-top
   The old King sits ;
He is now so old and gray
   He's nigh lost his wits.
With a bridge of white mist
   Columbkill he crosses,
On his stately journeys
   From Slieveleague to Rosses ;
Or going up with music
   On cold starry nights,
To sup with the Queen
   Of the gay Northern Lights.

They stole little Bridget
   For seven years long ;
When she came down again
   Her friends were all gone.
They took her lightly back,
   Between the night and morrow,
They thought that she was fast asleep,
   But she was dead with sorrow.
They have kept her ever since
   Deep within the lake,
On a bed of flag-leaves,
   Watching till she wake.

By the craggy hill-side,
   Through the mosses bare,
They have planted thorn-trees
   For pleasure here and there.

Is any man so daring
  As dig up them in spite,
He shall find their sharpest thorns
  In his bed at night.

Up the airy mountain,
  Down the rushy glen,
We daren't go a-hunting
  For fear of little men ;
Wee folk, good folk,
  Trooping all together ;
Green jacket, red cap,
  And white owl's feather !

WILLIAM ALLINGHAM.

THE MAIDS OF ELFIN-MERE.

'TWAS when the spinning-room was here,
Came Three Damsels clothed in white,
With their spindles every night ;
Two and one, and Three fair Maidens,
Spinning to a pulsing cadence,
Singing songs of Elfin-Mere ;
Till the eleventh hour was told,
Then departed through the wold.
    Years ago, and years ago ;
    And the tall reeds sigh as the wind doth blow.

Three white Lilies, calm and clear,
And they were loved by every one ;
Most of all, the Parson's son,
Listening to their gentle singing,

Felt his heart go from him, clinging,
Round these Maids of Elfin-Mere;
Sued each night to make them stay,
Sadden'd when they went away.
 Years ago, and years ago ;
 And the tall reeds sigh as the wind doth blow.

Hands that shook with love and fear,
Dared put back the village clock,—
Flew the spindle, turn'd the rock,
Flow'd the song with subtle rounding,
Till the false "eleven" was sounding ;
Then these Maids of Elfin-Mere
Swiftly, softly, left the room,
Like three doves on snowy plume.
 Years ago, and years ago ;
 And the tall reeds sigh as the wind doth blow.

One that night who wander'd near
Heard lamentings by the shore,
Saw at dawn three stains of gore
In the waters fade and dwindle.
Nevermore with song and spindle
Saw we Maids of Elfin-Mere.
The Pastor's Son did pine and die ;
Because true love should never lie.
 Years ago, and years ago ;
 And the tall reeds sigh as the wind doth blow.

WILLIAM ALLINGHAM.

Epilogue.

FAREWELL TO THE FAIRIES.

FAREWELL rewards and fairies,
   Good housewives now may say,
For now foul sluts in dairies
   Do fare as well as they.
And though they sweep their hearths no less
   Than maids were wont to do,
Yet who of late, for cleanliness,
   Finds sixpence in her shoe?

Lament, lament, old abbeys,
   The fairies lost command ;
They did but change priests' babies,
   But some have changed your land ;
And all your children sprung from thence
   Are now grown Puritans ;
Who live as changelings ever since,
   For love of your domains.

At morning and at evening both,
   You merry were and glad,
So little care of sleep or sloth
   These pretty ladies had ;
When Tom came home from labour,
   Or Cis to milking rose,
Then merrily went their tabour,
   And nimbly went their toes.

Witness those rings and roundelays
   Of theirs, which yet remain,
Were footed in Queen Mary's days
   On many a grassy plain ;

But since of late Elizabeth,
   And later, James came in,
They never danced on any heath
   As when the time hath been.

By which we note the fairies
   Were of the old profession,
Their songs were Ave Maries,
   Their dances were procession :
But now, alas ! they all are dead,
   Or gone beyond the seas ;
Or farther for religion fled,
   Or else they take their ease.

A tell-tale in their company
   They never could endure,
And whoso kept not secretly
   Their mirth, was punished sore ;
It was a just and Christian deed
   To pinch such black and blue :
Oh, how the Commonwealth doth need
   Such justices as you.

                    RICHARD CORBET.

FAIRY SONG.

HAVE ye left the greenwood lone ?
Are your steps for ever gone ?
Fairy King and Elfin Queen,
Come ye to the sylvan scene,
From your dim and distant shore,
              Never more ?

Shall the pilgrim never hear
With a thrill of joy and fear,
In the hush of moonlight hours,
Voices from the folded flowers,
Faint sweet flute-notes as of yore,
              Never more ?

"Mortal ! ne'er shall bowers of earth
Hear again our midnight mirth :
By our brooks and dingles green
Since unhallow'd steps have been,
Ours shall thread the forests hoar
              Never more.

Ne'er on earthborn lily's stem
Will we hang the dewdrop's gem ;
Ne'er shall reed or cowslip's head
Quiver to our dancing tread,
By sweet fount or murmuring shore,
              Never more !"

                      FELICIA HEMANS.

AN INVOCATION.

By the Moon-Queen's mystic light,
By the hush of holy night,
By the woodland deep and green,
By the starlight's silver sheen,
By the zephyr's whisper'd spell,
Brooding Powers Invisible,
Faërie Court and Elfin Throng,
Unto whom the groves belong,
And by Laws of ancient date,
Found in Scrolls of Faërie Fate,

Stream and fount are dedicate,
Wheresoe'er your feet to-day,
Far from haunts of men may stray,
We adjure you, stay no more,
Exiles on an alien shore,
But with spells of magic birth
Once again make glad the earth !

Here in glade and dingle sweet
Ye may find a snug retreat :
Can ye wish for softer bed
Than the moss that here is spread ?
Here the mavis' voice is heard,
Every late and early bird ;
Many a tendril's slender string
Here is fit for fairy swing ;
Purling brooks and founts that play
Make sweet music night and day ;
In the lakes that stedfast lie
Under Heaven's eternal eye,
The blown lilies, waiting, float,
Each will serve as elfin boat ;
Tender as a harper's string
Is the low wind's lute-playing ;
Never do the evening dews
Nectar to the flowers refuse :
Who shall find a fairer spot ?
Linger, fairies, linger not !

*   *   *   *

Still the woods are dark and lonely ;
There the throstle calleth only—
There alone the throstle calleth
As the silent twilight falleth ;
All the magic spells are broken,
All the ancient charms unspoken.

Who to human tongues shall teach
That forgotten fairy speech,
By whose aid the world of old
Did with Nature commune hold ?
'Tis the pride of human hearts
Whence the gentle fay departs !
Ye who now their loss deplore,
Ye who would their reign restore,
Know that fervent faith and worth
Elfin blessings bring to earth ;
Purest thoughts are brightest chrism
In the mystical baptism,
Which to those elected duly
Lifts the veil, revealing truly
Elfin worlds in 'rapt clairvoyance,
Elfin marvels, Elfin joyance,
Elfin vistas, Elfin vision,
Elfin voices, dreams Elysian,
Fay-built isles and seas that be
Glamour all and gramarye.
Where shall point the Elfin wing ?
Worlds of pure imagining ;
Then where virtue rules the heart
Thence the Fairies ne'er depart !

PHILIP DAYRE.

Printed by WALTER SCOTT, Felling, Newcastle-on-Tyne.

THE CAMELOT SERIES.

CLOTH, CUT OR UNCUT EDGES.

New Comprehensive Edition of Favourite Prose Works.

Edited by ERNEST RHYS.

In SHILLING Monthly Volumes, Crown 8vo.

VOLUMES ALREADY ISSUED.

ROMANCE OF KING ARTHUR.

THOREAU'S WALDEN.

CONFESSIONS OF AN ENGLISH OPIUM-EATER.

LANDOR'S CONVERSATIONS.

PLUTARCH'S LIVES.

SIR T. BROWNE'S RELIGIO MEDICI, &c.

ESSAYS AND LETTERS OF P. B. SHELLEY.

PROSE WRITINGS OF SWIFT.

MY STUDY WINDOWS.

GREAT ENGLISH PAINTERS.

LORD BYRON'S LETTERS.

ESSAYS BY LEIGH HUNT.

LONGFELLOW'S PROSE.

GREAT MUSICAL COMPOSERS.

MARCUS AURELIUS.

SPECIMEN DAYS IN AMERICA.

WHITE'S NATURAL HISTORY OF SELBORNE.

CAPTAIN SINGLETON.

ESSAYS BY MAZZINI.

PROSE WRITINGS OF HEINRICH HEINE.

JOSHUA REYNOLDS' DISCOURSES.

THE LOVER, and other Papers of Steele and Addison.

BURNS'S LETTERS.

VOLSUNGA SAGA.

SARTOR RESARTUS.

SELECT WRITINGS OF EMERSON.

SENECA'S MORALS.

DEMOCRATIC VISTAS.

Life of LORD HERBERT.

ENGLISH PROSE.

The Series is issued in two styles of Binding—Red Cloth, Cut Edges; and Dark Blue Cloth, Uncut Edges. Either Style, 1s.

London: WALTER SCOTT, 24 Warwick Lane, Paternoster Row.

Windsor Series of Poetical Anthologies.

Printed on Antique Paper. Crown 8vo. Bound in Blue Cloth, each with suitable Emblematic Design on Cover, Price 3/6. Also in various Calf and Morocco Bindings.

Women's Voices. An Anthology of the most Characteristic Poems by English, Scotch, and Irish Women. Edited by Mrs. William Sharp.

Sonnets of this Century. With an Exhaustive and Critical Essay on the Sonnet. Edited by William Sharp.

The Children of the Poets. An Anthology from English and American Writers of Three Centuries. Edited by Professor Eric S. Robertson.

Sacred Song. A Volume of Religious Verse. Selected and arranged, with Notes, by Samuel Waddington.

A Century of Australian Song. Selected and Edited by Douglas B. W. Sladen, B.A., Oxon.

Jacobite Songs and Ballads. Selected and Edited, with Notes, by G. S. Macquoid.

Irish Minstrelsy. Edited, with Notes and Introduction, by H. Halliday Sparling.

The Sonnets of Europe. A Volume of Translations. Selected and arranged, with Notes, by Samuel Waddington.

Early English and Scottish Poetry. Selected and Edited, with Introduction and Notes, by H. Macaulay Fitzgibbon.

Ballads of the North Countrie. Edited, with Introduction, by Graham R. Tomson.

Songs and Poems of the Sea. An Anthology of Poems Descriptive of the Sea. Edited by Mrs. William Sharp.

Songs and Poems of Fairyland. An Anthology of English Fairy Poetry. Selected and arranged, with an Introduction, by Arthur Edward Waite.

London: WALTER SCOTT, 24 Warwick Lane, Paternoster Row.

Square 8vo, Price Sixpence.

PARENTAL COMMANDMENTS

Or, Warnings to Parents

ON THE PHYSICAL, INTELLECTUAL, AND
MORAL TRAINING OF THEIR CHILDREN.

The Lancet.—"Very sensible advice—terse, interesting, instructive, well considered and accurate."

Newcastle Chronicle.—"If studied and acted upon, would quickly be a more beneficial revolution of society than all the hosts of Social reformers can ever hope to accomplish."

Oscar Wilde.—"Charming little book—full of wit and wisdom."

J. A. Froude.—"It contains more sense in a short space than any book which I have read for a long time."

Dr. Samuel Smiles.—"Capital book, full of sound advice, should be widely read."

London: WALTER SCOTT. 24 Warwick Lane, Paternoster Row.